God Is <u>NOT</u> on Vacation!

One Man's Mission to Feed HIS Sheep

David Timothy, a.k.a. The SoupMan

©2010—2011 David Timothy, Dallas, Texas

All rights reserved. Copyright includes but is not limited to printed books, electronic media, and email transmissions.

Registered trademarks, trademarks, service mark, and copyrights in this book are the property of their respective owners.

Excerpts and quotes from this book may be used by individuals without permission from the author.

For permission to use excerpts or quotations in commercial work, email David Timothy at david@soupmobile.org

ISBN 1453600671
EAN-13 is 9781453600672

10 9 8 7 6 5 4 3 2 1

Table of Contents

Dedication

Special Thanks

Kudos

Author's Note

Chapter 1: Got Milk?

Chapter 2: Conventional Wisdom!

Chapter 3: Christmas---For the Homeless???

Chapter 4: The Perfect Storm!

Chapter 5: <u>After</u> the Perfect Storm!

Chapter 6: Take a Vacation Dude!

Chapter 7: The Great Divide!

Chapter 8: Moments that Touched My Heart!

Chapter 9: The Mayor of Boxville!

Chapter 10: Is This <u>Your</u> Moment?

Dedication

This book is dedicated to my dear wife Shana. When we were married on October 18, 2008, I felt like the most blessed man on the planet. Now, many years later, I still feel the same way. Shana is my passion, my joy, my soulmate and my SoupGirl.

There are no pretentions about Shana. She is a bouncing ball of love and kindness. She wears her heart on her sleeve and loves both people and animals. She volunteers at the SoupMobile helping the homeless and is also active in animal rescues. I often joke that her passion for helping others makes me look like a slacker, but I think it's absolutely true!

>Thank you Shana for believing in me!
>Thank you for championing my dreams!
>Thank you for loving me!

I'm sure there is a more wonderful wife out there, **<u>JUST NOT ON THIS PLANET!</u>**

Signed, David Timothy, a.k.a. **<u>Your</u>** SoupMan

Special Thanks

My grateful thanks to the wonderful group of individuals who helped make this book a reality--- LeAnne Baird, Linda Graf, Lon Ricker and Kirby Timmons. Without you this book would not have been possible.

Thank you for your diligence, patience and attention to detail as you all brought your special editing talents to the table.

Blessings to you for investing your talent, your time and your energy in helping this book come to fruition.

Working with you on the book has been my honor and privilege.

May the Lord bless you & yours.

Signed, David Timothy, a.k.a. The SoupMan

Kudos!!!

Kudos to my extraordinary staff! They are the true heart & soul of the SoupMobile. A group of men and women that I am proud to have as members of the SoupMobile Family.

Cynthia L: A true woman of God. She has a kind and generous heart and is constantly reaching out to the ones Jesus called the 'least of these.' She has been with the SoupMobile from the very beginning.

Iting C: An incredible woman with a passion for Jesus. The message on her answering machine says, 'If this is an emergency—call Jesus.' She is a blessing to everyone she meets.

Kirby T: A man we affectionately call the Kirbster. He is an inspiration and blesses each and every one of us with his kindness and gentle spirit. His wise counsel and sage advice are a blessing as he joins us in going about 'Our Fathers Work.'

LeAnne B: Our Community Outreach leader. She is kind and loving and continually reaches out to the homeless in Dallas with her special brand of giving. She has an amazing passion for helping others.

Linda G: She blesses us each day with her smile, her laughter and her love for the Lord. Her commitment to the mission of the SoupMobile is second to none. And oh, can she make some great chocolate chip cookies!

Lon R: A man of caring & compassion. A man with a passion for 'Feeding HIS Sheep.' A man of vision and an extraordinary ability to think out of the box. A man I am proud to call my friend.

Chef Lou K: Our fair lady of the kitchen. A chef who serves up more than wonderful food---she serves up love, caring and compassion for the less fortunate in our community.

Mack C: The Mayor of Boxville. A friend for life and a man with a heart of gold. A man whose work ethic is off the charts. A man whose word is his bond. A man for all time.

Michael M: He is known as the 'PeaceMaker.' He brings people together in our common mission of helping the poor. A man of kindness, forgiveness and mercy. A true man of God.

Sandra D: An amazing blessing to her fellowman. A woman of God and an accomplished gospel singer. A heart as big as Texas and a powerful commitment to making a positive difference in the lives of the homeless.

Chef Thomas W: A chef beyond compare. He doesn't just cook up great food, he cooks it up with that magic ingredient---Love! He is a true blessing to the SoupMobile and to his fellowman.

Tom P: Our ace Delivery Driver. He can handle a vehicle like A.J. Foyt and can shine happiness into your heart faster than any race car driver. A man of integrity, kindness and compassion.

Author's Note

This book is really all about God.

The book interweaves my story, the story of the homeless and the story of the SoupMobile. But make no mistake about it, this book is about the wonder and majesty of the Lord.

In the book I tell of many of my own personal struggles. I describe how I dealt with a childhood of hunger and poverty. I also talk about the time in my adult life when it became 'all about me' and I convey the culture shock of becoming a caregiver. I go on to talk about my role with the SoupMobile.

I share my story because it's my way of showing the reader that the God of the Red Sea is alive and well. As you read the book, I urge you **to continually look beyond my story** and focus on God's love, caring and compassion for each and every one of us.

As author, my name may be on the cover of the book but God's handprint is on each and every page. This book is not about me---it's all about HIM.

May the Lord bless you & yours!

Signed, David Timothy, a.k.a. The SoupMan

Chapter 1
Got Milk?

Milk—It does a body good.
> The National Dairy Council

2,000 years ago a child was born in Bethlehem. As this child grew into manhood he became quite revolutionary for his time. He did some things that no one else had ever done before. He did miraculous things like turning water into wine. Then he topped that by walking on the water. He went around laying hands on people and healing them. Then he bumped that up a notch and started healing people that he had never seen by simply speaking the Word. Not satisfied with that, he began raising people from the dead. Even that was not enough as he raised himself from the dead. His name---Jesus!

The Bible says that Jesus came that we would have life and have it more abundantly.

Fast forward two thousand years and another child was born in Detroit, Michigan. That child wasn't very revolutionary and he didn't do anything miraculous. That child was me—David Timothy. My childhood years were ones of poverty and lack. That abundance Jesus had promised was nowhere to be found. There wasn't a lot of food in our home and hunger was a constant companion. Abundance??? Well I certainly didn't see any. Back then I didn't know who Jesus was and frankly I didn't care. I was more interested in where the next meal was coming from.

As kids I vividly remember when my older brother Gene was invited to dinner at the home of one of the rich kids from school. Mom secretly dreaded sending him to their house. She knew my brother was out of his league and she was fearful that he would be embarrassed by these rich people. She made him take a bath and dressed him in his best clothes, such as they were. Off went Gene to have dinner with his rich school yard friend. A couple of hours later, he came home and told us the most amazing, most astounding and most incredible story that we had ever heard in the few short years we had lived on the planet.

Gene told us how they had different 'courses' during the meal. We had no idea what that meant. He explained how they started with a salad, graduated to the main course and then finished with ice cream and pie for desert. We listened in awe as he told us how the main course actually consisted of different kinds of meat, vegetables, hot dinner rolls, butter and even some kind of sauce to pour over the whole thing. We listened intently as he told us how they even had a different fork for the salad and another one for the main course. It all sounded like something out of science fiction movie.

Many times dinner at our home was a sandwich that consisted of two pieces of white bread layered with butter and sugar sprinkled on it. Sometimes if we were lucky we would sit down to dinner and there would be one large bowl sitting in the middle of the table. In that one bowl was everything we would be eating at that meal. All mixed into one---a goulash of some kind. That bowl was filled with whatever my mother could scrape together to come up with some kind of meal. She served a true 'one course' meal.

Different 'courses', ha! Until my brother described what that meant we didn't have a clue of what 'courses' were. As we sat there listening to my brother describe the meal at his rich friends house our jaws hung down in absolute wonder. We were held spellbound as he breathlessly told us every detail.

Then he told us something that was almost impossible to grasp. Something so astonishing, so fantastic and so far beyond our wildest comprehension, that we only believed it because my brother had a reputation for being so honest. Gene told us that at dinner he was allowed to drink all the milk he wanted. We gasped! That simply was not possible---all the milk he wanted! At our home milk was a rarity. Only on special occasions was it there for us and even when it was we knew that one glass was the absolute limit. Unlimited milk! All he could drink! Oh my gosh, my brother had hit the mother lode.

As a child I thought eating breakfast cereal with water poured on it was normal. Milk on cereal? Well sure, that was something we would see on commercials on TV advertising cereal, but that was the extent of that fantasy. So here I am over a half century later and I still eat my cereal with water poured on top of it. After Shana and I were married in October of 2008 she literally stopped and gasped the first time she saw me pour water on my cereal. She thought I was playing around. I wasn't---it's just the way I had always eaten it. Old habits die hard.

You might be wondering if I am bitter about my childhood of hunger. Am I mad at that Jesus guy who was born 2,000 years before me and said that he came so that I would have abundance. On the surface you would think I have every right to be angry. Gosh, I was just an innocent kid and it looked like God had taken off on a big Vacation. Oh sure, he said he sent his son so that I would have abundant life, but the reality seemed much different. I mean like gee whiz, don't you think he could have taken a few moments and told one of his Angels to make sure I got enough food. He could have just waved his little pinkie finger and I could have had all the food I needed. But no such luck for this kid. So am I bitter?

Actually I'm grateful. Grateful? For what? For hunger, for lack, for fear of the next meal not being there. Grateful---how could that be? Well let me tell you where I'm coming from. What good can come out of a childhood of hunger? Not much one would think. But think again. Could it be possible that a child suffering hunger could actually be a good thing? Could it be possible that the hunger I suffered as a child would turn out to be a blessing? It seems it has. So hang onto your hat and let me give you the lowdown.

My name is David Timothy but on the streets of Dallas the homeless call me the SoupMan. We feed and shelter the homeless through our charity called the SoupMobile. We serve an astounding 200,000 meals per year and we shelter them through our venture called SoupMobile Village. (More about the Village later). So now the question is---what am I doing as an adult feeding the homeless? Even though I suffered hunger as a child, I was never homeless and I never knew any homeless people. All I knew about was hunger, not homelessness. However it seems God knew there would be a connection. He used the hunger I suffered as a child as one of the motivating factors to get me to feed the homeless.

If you are homeless your number one priority each day is to find food. It turns out that the hunger I experienced as a child has given me a tremendous compassion for the homeless who struggle to find food every day. And even though it seemed like God was on Vacation when I was a child, it turns out he was just planting a seed. He used my childhood hunger to plant a seed of compassion in me for the homeless. That seed would lay dormant for over a half century. During that half century God patiently waited until he knew the time was right for that seed to sprout. I find his patience absolutely amazing.

God ordains that some children will be prodigies. They are born with an extraordinary talent or ability. As children their gifts are obvious. As a child growing up in Detroit, Michigan I exhibited no such special gifts. At best I was average. I was just a kid trying to get by.

It seems that God has this amazing ability to plan ahead. Who knew! In my case he planned 50 years into the future. And even though I didn't know it, he spent that 50 years training me to be an <u>adult</u> prodigy. He was training me to be the SoupMan. Believe it or not, it does take a unique set of skills to be the SoupMan. It's not just about handing out food. I have to be equally comfortable in the boardroom as I would be at midnight under a bridge in South Dallas visiting a homeless encampment. I have to meet with high dollar donors and be equally adept at meeting with a gang leader to ask his permission to feed the homeless on his turf. I have to be an able leader but also a willing follower. I have to be confident in my own abilities but be humble enough to know that it's Jesus who is leading the way.

Let me stress that I don't take any credit for any of the SoupMan type talents or skills that I have. They are all gifts from God himself. They are **HIS** skills, **HIS** talents and **HIS** abilities. They are not mine. At best I only have them on loan from the Lord.

This shows you just how smart God is. Not only could he plant a seed that would take 50 years to sprout but during that time he patiently taught me what I would need to know to operate effectively as the SoupMan. Can you believe it? He spent 50 years grooming me for my life's work which is feeding and caring for the homeless. I don't know whether to be flattered that God gave me 50 years of hands on training or embarrassed that it took me 50 years to get all the lessons! In any event it turns out that God knew exactly what he was doing when he let me suffer hunger as a child. He knew that only by my suffering hunger first hand could I have a true compassion and empathy for the homeless.

So am I bitter that I suffered hunger as a child? No, I am truly grateful. Now as an adult and as the SoupMan I am privileged and honored to be able to feed the homeless. And while I'm not rich when it comes to money, my life is one of richness and an abundance of love, caring and compassion. So while on the surface a hungry child may not seem like a good thing, in my own life it turned out to be a blessing beyond comprehension.

2,000 years ago a child was born in Bethlehem. He came that I would have life and have it more abundantly. He kept his promise!

Chapter 2
Conventional Wisdom!

If everybody else is doing it one way, there's a good chance you can find your niche by going in exactly the opposite direction. But be prepared for a lot of folks to wave you down and tell you you're headed the wrong way.

Sam Walton — Founder of Wal-Mart

Webster's Dictionary defines Conventional Wisdom as: 'The generally accepted belief, opinion, judgment, or prediction about a particular matter.'

The SoupMan defines Conventional Wisdom as: **'A bunch of hogwash.'**

Let's take a moment and travel back in time 2,000 years ago. Remember that Jesus guy I talked about in the first chapter of this book. Do you think that for one moment he followed the 'conventional wisdom' of the times? I don't think so! Remember this is the guy that turned water into wine, walked on the water, multiplied the loaves and the fishes, preached forgiveness, spoke of a loving God, healed the sick, raised people from the dead and then himself rose from the dead after three days. Does that sound like conventional wisdom to you? It's no wonder that the Pharisees of the day hated Jesus and plotted his death. Jesus literally went against everything the Pharisees believed and all known conventional wisdom of the day.

Whether Jesus was conventional or unconventional was of little concern to me as I was growing up in Detroit, Michigan. As I said earlier in this book I didn't know Jesus as a hungry child and I really didn't care. All I was concerned about was getting that next meal. However as an adult I have come to know Jesus and I think HE is pretty amazing. I think he is 'off the chain.' For you conventional folk that means Jesus is pretty cool. Some people might think its heresy to talk about Jesus that way. They think we should just talk about Jesus in low reverent tones. But let's try to put ourselves in Jesus' shoes.

We already know from the Bible he virtually went against all the conventional wisdom of the day. We know he was quite radical in many ways. How about that time he healed the servant of the Centurion by simply speaking the Word. Or what about him calling Lazurus out from the tomb after he had been dead for four days. And how about Jesus getting all excited and kicking the money changers out of the temple. So while I do deeply reverence Jesus, no matter how you slice the cake, he is pretty cool. That's my story and I'm sticking to it. So I figured if ignoring conventional wisdom was good enough for Jesus, it was good enough for me.

So completely disregarding conventional wisdom, on August 13, 2003 I started a non-profit charity called the SoupMobile---a mobile soupkitchen to feed the homeless in the Dallas area. It was an act of total madness. Conventional Wisdom said (and still says) you can't start a major soupkitchen or any major charity unless you have a deep pocket donor or are under the umbrella of a church. Fortunately I never got that memo. The only memo I did get was the one that said, "I *can do all things through Christ who strengthens me."* Philippians 4:13. So in August of 2003 the SoupMobile was born on a wing and a lot of prayers. It didn't matter that we had no money, no donors, no experience feeding the homeless, no permits, no mobile feeding van, no tax exempt status from the I.R.S., no sources of food, no deep pocket donors and no church to provide a safety umbrella. All that mattered was that Jesus himself said I can do all things through him. I mean like gee whiz, either we believe in the guy or not. There is no in between. You can't ride the fence when it comes to Jesus.

So with virtually nothing the SoupMobile was born in 2003. By the way before I go any further, let's talk about the word 'I'. It's not a word I like to use very often. I much prefer words like 'we', 'us', 'staff', and 'team.' So when I say 'I' started the SoupMobile in 2003 I really mean 'HIM', the ONE, yes Jesus. He was the one who led the way, moved mountains, parted the Red seas and I just followed in his footsteps and let him lead.

Some people think leadership is learned by taking special classes or attending college, but I think leadership is learned by following Jesus. By following HIM we learn to lead others. I don't know how good a leader I am but I do know who I will be following the rest of my life.

So back to the birth of the SoupMobile in 2003. In that first year of operation we served 5,000 meals to the homeless in the Dallas area. At the time we thought it was a lot. Now we serve more than 200,000 meals per years. Not bad for following a guy (Jesus) who disdained all conventional wisdom and got the Pharisees very upset.

But just like Jesus didn't stop by healing just one person, we didn't stop with just feeding the homeless. In addition to feeding the homeless the SoupMobile founded an amazing Christmas event in 2005 that is totally 'off the chain.' If you've been paying attention you already know what that phrase means. Each year the SoupMobile literally takes 500 homeless men and women right off the streets of Dallas and puts them up at the downtown Dallas Hyatt Regency Hotel for Christmas. They all get new clothes, fabulous gifts, lots of love and we hold a huge banquet in their honor. Most important is that when they wake up on Christmas Morning it's not in a cardboard box under some bridge, but in a warm safe bed at the Hyatt. Later in this book I'll tell you more about this magical Christmas event. But feeding the homeless 200,000 meals per year and even giving them the Christmas of their lives was not enough. In 2009 we again expanded our operation to include sheltering the homeless in a venture called <u>SoupMobile Village</u>.

Wow, are you hearing what I'm saying. In seven short years, with Jesus leading the way, we have come from absolutely nothing to becoming a major charity that feeds, shelters and puts on a one of a kind Christmas event that no one else in the entire nation is doing. The moral of this story is to choose wisely who you will follow. You can go the 'I can do all things through Christ' route or you can follow some other entity. It's your call.

So now you know we ignored conventional wisdom when the SoupMobile was born in 2003, but you don't know the WHY?

Why??? That's a question I get asked a lot. Why did I decide to devote my life to feeding and caring for the homeless? Well the short answer is to remind you of the hunger I suffered as a child. That in itself gave me compassion for the homeless who struggle to find food every day. But remember I was never homeless and I had never known or been exposed to homeless people. Truth be told, it's quite a leap from being a hungry child to devoting your entire life to feeding and caring for the homeless. Even stranger, I wasn't raised in a family or church environment that fed the homeless. I didn't even know anybody who had ever fed the homeless. In college I never took any courses about the homeless and even in the Army I never came across any homeless people.

So we are back to the **WHY???** Why devote my life-- my very being, to feeding and caring for the homeless. For the answer we will have to travel back in time to late 1980's.

For me that was a good time. I was doing fairly well in my business life. I wasn't rich or anything near rich but I was doing well. Business was good, I had a lot of friends, played a lot of golf, ate at the best restaurants in town and basically enjoyed living the good life. I thought I had 'arrived.' And wonder of wonders it was about to get even better. In 1989 I married a beautiful, healthy, vibrant young lady by the name of Peggy. She was a former cheerleader with an amazing upbeat personality and a real caring for her fellowman. Oh baby, I had hit the jackpot. Life was good---very good!

You won't believe how quickly it all came crashing down. To this day I still find it a little hard to comprehend. Literally within a few days of our marriage and saying our 'I Do's', Peggy started having physical difficulties. She was having trouble with her balance and felt tired. Completely the opposite of the healthy woman that I had married just a few days before. We headed off to the Doctor and got the shock of our lives. Peggy had Multiple Sclerosis. This could not be—no way it could be true—not M.S.—not Peggy. We got a second opinion. Same diagnosis—M.S.

Nooooooooooooooooooooooooooooooo, this simply could not be. 'I' had been living the good life. 'I' was prosperous. 'I' ate at the finest restaurants. 'I' was having fun playing golf. 'I' had hit the jackpot and married this vibrant and amazing woman. Notice all the 'I's'.

Somehow over the years life had become all about **ME**. Maybe I was overreacting to the hunger I suffered as a child. Maybe I was compensating for growing up poor. Maybe I thought that I was owed something. Somehow I had gone from a innocent child gasping in wonder as my older brother described how he could drink all the milk he wanted at his rich friends house, to a selfish, self centered adult. Whatever the reason, my life had become all about ME. I basically lived my life just for me. Living my life for anyone else, let alone devoting my life to feeding and caring for the homeless, was the last thing on my mind. Oh sure, I had read in the Bible about how Jesus said 'Feed My Sheep.' But surely he wasn't referring to me. Yep, Jesus was cool. I read his words, I believed in him, I just didn't think he actually meant for ME to 'love my neighbor as myself.'

And what about Peggy? Oh my, what a cruel twist of fate for her. She was the one who really suffered. It seemed so unfair. I was the selfish one. She was the giving one. I was the one who lived my life for myself. She was the one who lived her life for others. Well God must have been pretty unhappy about my self-centered lifestyle because overnight my life was literally turned topsy turvy. I was now married to a wife with Multiple Sclerosis. A disease for which there is no cure. A progressive disease that can and does get worse for many M.S. patients.

Overnight my title changed from husband to caregiver. Talk about culture shock. I went from being the toast of the town getting served at the finest restaurants to the one who was doing the serving. I had to go from being a self centered person to trying to learn how to be a caring, loving and compassionate caregiver. My world was literally turned upside down.

Early on in the disease process I got the scare of my life. Shortly after getting Peggy's M.S. diagnosis I started researching the disease. Since I was going to be her caregiver, I wanted to know as much as I could about M.S. so I would know how to best care for Peggy as she dealt with disease. There was a wealth of information but much of it was conflicting. By that I mean, things that worked for some M.S. patients didn't work for others. Things that hindered some people with M.S. had no negative effect on others. It was confusing to say the least.

That confusion almost cost Peggy her life and did give me the scare of my short life as a caregiver. As part of dealing with the aches and pains of M.S., Peggy liked to take long hot baths to help relieve the pain. I would have to help her into the tub, fill up the hot water and then later drain the tub and help her out. This in itself was not an easy process. M.S. patients who don't have the complete use of their legs and are weak in arm strength need help just doing the most basic things. Early on these hot baths had a very therapeutic effect on Peggy. However as time went on she was becoming more sensitive to heat. For some M.S. patients hot temperatures and hot baths can be debilitating. Somehow in the progression of the disease Peggy went from being helped by a hot bath to it almost costing her life.

One evening I was putting Peggy into her hot bath just like we had always done. We didn't know that heat was becoming her enemy. She had always responded so well to the hot baths. That night was different. I put Peggy in the tub, ran the hot water so the bathtub was almost filled to the top and Peggy started to relax. Normally she would spend about 30 minutes in the bath and then call me and I would help her get out. I would always leave the bathroom door slightly ajar so I could hear her when she called. That particular night I got her into the bath and went to make a phone call. The phone was only about 20 feet from the bathroom, so with the door ajar I could easily hear her when she called to come out. Somehow that phone call went a little longer than I had planned and about 40 minutes later when I hung up Peggy still had not called for me. I wasn't concerned because we had done the bath tub thing many times. But tonight would be different.

When I finished the phone call I went to the bathroom door, lightly knocked and called to Peggy asking if she were ready to come out. Strangely there was no answer. I knocked again and called a little more loudly asking if she was ready. There was still no answer. Now I started to get concerned. I opened the door a crack, looked in and got the shock of my life. Peggy's head was slumped under the water and she was not moving. I could see that her lips were blue and she was lifeless. She had become incapacitated by the heat of the water. I flew into action. I instinctively knew there was no time to drain the bathtub and get her out the normal way. I knew I had to get her out of that tub and start CPR immediately. There was not a second to waste.

There was only one quick way to get her out. Standing on the outside of the tub I would have to bend over, reach in, put my arms under her and do a dead lift. This would be impossible. Think about it! It wasn't like reaching into the tub and picking up a little baby. Peggy weighed about 140 lbs at the time and I would have no leverage whatsoever in lifting her. Plus she was limp and wet and there would be no easy way to get a firm hold on her. I would be lifting almost 85 percent of my own body weight. Still I knew a dead lift was the only way. I looked up at the ceiling and said "God---give me strength." So standing outside the tub I reached down, slid my arms under her limp body and lifted with all my might. It one fluid motion I had her up and out of the tub and on the floor.

It was a super human lift. There is no possible way it could be done. You could give me a million dollars and I still could not do that lift. Even for a <u>very</u> strong person it would be an incredibly difficult lift. It was God's strength pouring through me that made that lift possible. I called for his help and he came through.

Getting Peggy out of the bathtub was only half the battle. She wasn't breathing. I had learned CPR in the army and started giving it to her. I worked on her for what seemed like hours but I know it was only minutes. There was no response. I was going to call 911. Instantly a powerful thought came into my head. It said, 'if you take the time to make the call you will lose her.' I knew who that thought was from (God) and I knew it was right. She already wasn't responding and it would take precious extra minutes to leave her, go to the phone and give the operator all the information they needed to get the paramedics to us. It was literally a do or die situation. So I obeyed that thought in my head and did NOT call 911. I kept working on Peggy. I tried every CPR trick I had learned in the Army. Still no movement from Peggy. I was tempted again to call 911 but that powerful thought came back into my head saying, 'if you take the time to make the call you will lose her.'

In sheer desperation I looked up to the ceiling and screamed, 'I WILL NOT ALLOW DEATH IN THIS HOUSE.' It was a guttural howling primal scream that came from deep inside me. I kept working on

Peggy and within about 10 seconds of me screaming, 'I will not allow death in this house,' Peggy started to stir. Oh praise God, miracles of miracles, she was alive. I continued the CPR and soon she was breathing normally and getting color back into her face. We had gone to the edge of the abyss and come back.

I dried her off and got her up into the bed. I fed her warm chicken broth and some orange juice. I asked her if she wanted to go to the hospital. She said no--- and that she was okay. I gently pressed her on the issue but I could see she was fine. I figured a trip to the hospital would only compound the trauma she had already been though that night. I was learning early on that caregivers have to make some tough decisions. It turned out that NOT going to the hospital was the right decision. She was okay and just needed to rest. I covered her with blankets and told her to get some sleep. In a few minutes she fell fast asleep and for the next few hours I never moved from her bedside. I watched her every breath. Well, that should have been the end of the story, but there was more.

When Peggy woke up a few hours later, I asked her how she was and she said fine. She then asked me to slide up closer to the bed as she had something she wanted to tell me. To this day what she said still sends shivers down my spine. She said that as I had been giving her CPR, her spirit had already left her body and that she was in the room watching me working on her. She went on to say that her spirit was getting ready to leave the room when she heard me scream, 'I will not allow death in this house.' She said she heard those words and immediately came back into her body. I was stunned! God had been right---if I had taken the time to call 911, I would have lost her.

For the next 15 years I had a ringside seat as I watched Peggy go from being a former vibrant cheerleader to a bedridden invalid. For the next decade and a half I devoted my life to caring for Peggy. I gave it all up---the successful business, the fancy cars, my beloved golf and fancy restaurants. I left it all behind to care for Peggy. As part of my own personal journey I turned back to Jesus and the Bible. Now instead of just reading the words of Jesus, I had to start living them. Over the next 15 years God began transforming me from a self-indulgent person to someone who would be willing to serve. The ironic thing is that if the situation had been reversed I know Peggy would have devoted her life to caring for me. The big difference would have been that she would not have had a huge learning curve like I did. She was already totally equipped to love and care for me. Remember I was the selfish one and she was the giving one. She didn't just read the words of Jesus—she lived them.

Fifteen years after hearing that initial diagnosis of Multiple Sclerosis the universe dropped a bomb on us. Peggy died. She passed away in her sleep on her 48th birthday. I cannot begin to tell you what a complete and utter shock it was. While Peggy did have Multiple Sclerosis and while she was virtually bedridden, the Doctors were confident that her life was not in any immediate danger. They had told me in confidence that she would certainly live another 10 years and if there were advances in medical science, much longer. In my first book titled, 'Is God On Vacation!', I talk more about Peggy and her passing but suffice it to say that her sudden death was devastating.

For a long time after her death I experienced incredible guilt. I had stood guard for 15 years protecting her from anything I thought would cause her life to be even more difficult than it already was. I had cared for her every need. I had learned not only to be a caregiver but to be kind and loving. What happened that night she died in her sleep?

Where was I? For 15 years I had faithfully watched over her and cared for her. That bathtub incident had galvanized me and for the next 15 years I watched her like a hawk. Then it seemed as if I had taken one night off. I was racked by guilt for not awakening and saving her. Looking back I now know there was nothing I could have done but at the time my guilt was overwhelming.

So let's go back to the question. **<u>WHY?</u>** Why did I decide to start the SoupMobile? Why did I decide to devote my life to feeding and caring for the homeless?

Well clearly the hunger I suffered as a child was a push in the right direction. But on its own that would not have been enough. Just being hungry as a child would not have been enough incentive for me to devote my life to feeding and caring for the homeless. God knew I had developed into a selfish, self centered adult that was only interested in my own needs. He needed something else besides my childhood of hunger to get my attention. Well get it he did during my 15 year odyssey with Peggy.

I don't think God caused Peggy to get M.S., but I do think God used it to mold and transform me. That 15 year transformation <u>COMBINED</u> with the hunger I suffered as a child is the answer to the 'WHY' of me devoting my life to the homeless.

And just so there is no doubt, let's clear up something right now. I don't think I'm anything special. I am a sinner just like the Bible says in Romans 3:23: *"We have all sinned and come short of the glory of God."* Am I different from the guy that began that 15 year odyssey? Yes I can truthfully say I am. But have I arrived? Definitely not! Years ago I thought I had 'arrived', but I was wrong. I won't be making that mistake again. There is only one that has 'arrived.' Yes HIM, the ONE, Jesus!

Chapter 3
Christmas---
For the Homeless???

Christmas is doing a little something '<u>extra</u>' for someone.
>Charles Schulz,
>Peanuts Comic Strip Writer

Did you know that some people don't agree with Charles Schulz—author of the above quote. In fact, not only are they not willing to do something '<u>extra</u>' for the homeless at Christmas, they aren't willing to do anything at all. Somehow they have it in their heads that the homeless are not deserving of a special Christmas.

At one time in my life I was one of those people. I was more concerned about how wonderful my **own** Christmas would be. Whether or not the homeless were deserving of a great Christmas was of little concern to me. After some big time nudging from the Lord, I now look at Christmas for the homeless in a whole different light.

Tell a survivor of hurricane Katrina that became homeless by an act of nature that they are not deserving of a special Christmas. Tell a homeless mother who had to take her children and run for her life because her husband abused her, that she is not deserving. Tell a homeless man who got laid off from his job and lost everything, that he is not deserving. Tell a homeless military veteran who came back from the war to find his job gone, that he is not deserving. Homeless people not deserving of a blessed Christmas???

I guarantee---yes *guarantee*--- that Jesus believes the homeless **are** deserving of a special Christmas. And he ought to know. Look what happened to him 2,000 years ago. There was 'no room at the inn' for baby Jesus at Christmas. At the SoupMobile we believe Christmas should be a special time of the year for everyone---especially the homeless. We believe this so strongly, that I think I can safely say, we give the homeless of Dallas a **spectacular** Christmas every year.

So gather around little children (and you adults to) to hear a Christmas story that will flat out rock your world. Remember I told you in Chapter 2 of this book that when I started the SoupMobile in 2003 without any deep pocket donors or the support of a church, it was an act of madness. Well in 2005 I graduated from an act of <u>madness</u> to one of total <u>lunacy.</u>

In August of 2005 (a mere 24 months after the birth of the SoupMobile) I got an idea in my head that just seemed plumb crazy. I wanted to take 100 homeless men and women right off the streets and put them up at a fancy world class hotel for Christmas. They would all get new clothes, fabulous gifts, lots of love and we would hold a huge banquet in their honor. Most important is that when they awoke on Christmas morning it would be in a warm safe bed at the hotel---not in a cardboard box under some bridge. Oh my, just how do these ideas get into my head? I'm not totally sure but I think God sneaks them in when I'm not looking.

Okay, so this was just plain nuts. How was the SoupMobile going to put on a magical Christmas for 100 homeless people. We were a baby charity with no extra money for a Christmas extravaganza, no experience running this type of event, only a few months to Christmas and most important no commitment from a world class hotel (let alone any hotel) to host the event. Let's face it, we had every reason NOT to do the Christmas event. But there was that one small reason (okay—large reason) to push ahead and try to pull it off. Yes, the reason being that guy called Jesus!

Remember HIM! The Bible says that at Christmas 2,000 years ago there was no 'room at the inn' for the one called baby Jesus. How about in honor of Jesus we make 'room at the inn' for 100 of the homeless ones that Jesus calls the 'least of these.' We couldn't do anything about what happened back in Bethlehem 2,000 years ago when Jesus got locked out, but we could do something now. Or could we?

Just how do you find a fancy world class hotel that would be willing to take in 100 homeless people for Christmas? And how do you get the money to buy them all new clothes, fabulous gifts and hold a huge banquet in their honor. And where do you find the funds to pay for the hotel rooms when your SoupMobile budget is already strained to the breaking point. Well we put on our thinking cap on and came up with the answer. We would call upon one of our good friends for help. Better still we would call on our <u>best</u> friend---Jesus!

By Jove, that was the answer. We would turn to Jesus to part the Red Seas so that the SoupMobile could take 100 homeless people to a fancy world famous hotel for Christmas. After all, I hear that HE does know a thing or two about pulling off miracles! You heard about that turning water into wine thing, didn't you?

We figured the key to the whole Christmas deal was getting a world famous hotel on board. Doing that would give the event instant credibility with potential donors. More important it would give 100 homeless people the most magical Christmas of their lives. So with Jesus leading the way and working an incredible miracle, we got the world famous downtown Dallas Hyatt Regency Hotel to host the event. I write more about how this all went down in my first book but suffice to say that when Jesus gets involved things get done. So with the Hyatt on board, the donors stepped up to the plate and we put on a spectacular Christmas for 100 homeless men and women in December of 2005.

We called the event the <u>Christmas Angel Project</u>. Having successful pulled off this miracle event in 05 we decided to do it again in 2006. Only this time we took 200 homeless people to the Hyatt for Christmas. In 2007 we took 300; in 2008 we took 400; in 2009 we took 500 and as this book is going to print in 2010 we are taking 500 again. Moral of the story---when God puts an idea into your head, no matter how crazy it seems, he will give you the means to pull it off.

A little side note about the event. In 2010 we decided to change the name of the event from the Christmas Angel Project to <u>Celebrate Jesus.</u> Same event, just a new name. Why the name change you ask? We did it in honor of Jesus and to celebrate the true spirit of Christmas.

To my knowledge our Christmas event is a one of a kind in the entire nation. No one else is doing anything remotely like this for the homeless. The event has gotten so big that it draws major news coverage every year. Typically we get hundreds of volunteers every Christmas to come to the downtown Dallas Hyatt Regency and help us with the event. In 2009 we had over 1,500 volunteers. Like wow! The true spirit of Christmas is alive and well in Dallas, Texas.

In 2010 the world famous choir—The Vocal Majority is coming to the huge Christmas banquet that the SoupMobile throws each year for the homeless at the Hyatt. They will be entertaining both our 500 homeless guests and our volunteers. The Vocal Majority is truly a world class choir. They are Eleven-time Gold Medal Champions. They have performed all over the world to sold out audiences and even sang with the Mormon Tabernacle Choir. They have recorded an incredible body of musical work and performed with numerous ensembles including the Lettermen, Four Freshmen and the Oak Ridge boys. They have joined with many solo performers including Glen Campbell, Jimmy Dean, Jack Jones and Johnny Mann.

Do you want to take a guess on how much the Vocal Majority is charging us to come and sing for our guests this Christmas? Yep, you guessed it---Zero! Not one single penny. They are coming in the true spirit of Christmas. Just like Jesus, they are coming with a servant's heart. They are coming to use their God given musical talents to entertain the very ones that Jesus called the 'least of these.' So how does a baby charity like the SoupMobile get a world famous choir like the Vocal Majority to come to our Christmas event, let alone come for free. Ah well there's the rub---when you have a friend (a best friend) like Jesus helping you, 'all things are possible.'

Our Christmas event called <u>Celebrate Jesus</u> is all about treating our homeless guests like Kings & Queens. The Hyatt rolls out the Red Carpet in service as they treat each guest with kindness and compassion. The SoupMobile 'literally' rolls out its own RED CARPET. Let me give you a brief glimpse into the event. It all starts at 9:00AM on December 24th. Six huge gleaming buses pull up to the front door of the Hyatt loaded with our 500 homeless guests. Notice I said the front door---we don't bring our people in the back door. As they step off those buses, awaiting them is a 75ft Red Carpet---just like at the Academy Awards. Lining that Red Carpet are more than 1,000 volunteers who are clapping and cheering as the homeless make their walk into the hotel. It takes almost an hour for our 500 homeless people to make that walk because everyone is hugging them, patting them on the back and wishing them Merry Christmas. While they are walking the Red Carpet we have snow machines making snow and blowing it on everyone. At the same time we have a local high school band that is continually playing the Rocky theme song.

Oh my, the President of the United States could come to the Hyatt and NOT get a welcome as spectacular as the homeless get from the

SoupMobile. And that's just the beginning of Christmas at the Hyatt for our 500 guests. Later that day we hold a huge banquet in their honor. But this is not a typical banquet where we get served and we are the big muckety mucks. At the SoupMobile banquet we are the ones doing the serving and it's the homeless that are treated like Kings & Queens. Later in the evening they get special late night room service. It's a totally magical Christmas that our homeless guests will never forget.

It's also a Christmas that our volunteers will never forget. Volunteering at the Celebrate Jesus Christmas event is unlike any other volunteer opportunity you have even had. This much I can promise you. If you come and volunteer at our Celebrate Jesus Christmas event, it will NOT be the best volunteer opportunity of the year for you. What it will be is the best volunteer opportunity of your LIFE. Strong words I know, but when you see the tears in the eyes of our homeless guests and the smiles on their faces, your heart will be touched like it has never been touched before.

Every year at the event we get a lot of news coverage. Typically the Dallas Morning News covers the event as well as the local TV stations and even National Public Radio. The coverage is almost universally positive and uplifting. But a few years ago one of out of town reporters covering the event asked me a question that concerned me at the time. He said "why give them a great Christmas when they have to go back out on the streets when it's over." The simple answer is that the event gives the homeless <u>HOPE!</u> A homeless person living in a cardboard box under a bridge doesn't have much hope. He feels alone, valueless, deserted, left behind and has no hope that things will get better. Christmas with the SoupMobile helps change all that.

It all starts when they arrive at the hotel to find more than 1,000 cheering, clapping, welcoming volunteers waiting for them. That alone gives them hope that people do care about them. Then later that day when they attend the banquet and are treated like Kings & Queens they know that they are loved and they do have value. So yes, they are back on the streets after Christmas but now it's with something we all need---Hope.

As the SoupMan I get invited to speak at a lot of places about the issue of homelessness. I speak at churches, schools, Lions Clubs, Kiwanis Clubs, Boy Scouts, Girl Scouts and more. One of the things I do with my audience when I talk about the homeless and Christmas, is to ask them to close their eyes, put their hands over their hearts and think back to the best Christmas they ever had.

Maybe it was when they were little and the snow was softly falling and they got that favorite toy they had been hoping for. Maybe it was as a young adult and your future husband surprised you by asking you to marry him. Maybe you were older and it was a time when the whole family was able to gather together and celebrate the birth of baby Jesus. Whatever it was, it was a Christmas that was special and personal to you.

Then I ask the audience to slowly open their eyes. I gently remind them that the Christmas they had just remembered is long over but the fond memories remain. Those special memories will stay with them for a lifetime. So it is with our homeless guests. When the Celebrate Jesus Christmas event is long over, the fond memories remain. The kindness, the love and the Hope they received will stay with them for a lifetime. I think that's just how Jesus would want it to be.

So how about you? Would you like to experience the most magical Christmas of your entire lifetime? Would you like to make a difference in the life of a special homeless person at Christmas? Would you like to give a homeless person love, caring and Hope? If the answer is yes, come and volunteer at the SoupMobile's <u>Celebrate Jesus</u> Christmas event. You will change lives! But be prepared for your <u>own</u> life to be changed forever!

More information on the <u>Celebrate Jesus</u> Christmas event can be found at www.soupmobile.org

Chapter 4
The Perfect Storm!

Weather forecast for tonight: dark!
George Carlin---comedian

A 'Perfect Storm' is an event where a rare combination of events creates a disastrous situation. In 1997 Junger Sebastian wrote a book titled The Perfect Storm. A few years later it was turned into a movie starring George Clooney. The book told the true story of a monster storm that hit North America in October of 1991. It was the kind of storm that only happens once in every 100 years.

In August of 2009 I experienced my own Perfect Storm. However before I can tell you about that Perfect Storm I need to take you back to the birth of the SoupMobile in 2003. When we started the SoupMobile, its one and only mission was to feed the homeless. We started by serving 5,000 meals in that first year and now we serve more than 200,000 meals per year. Then in 2005 we expanded our mission by giving the homeless in Dallas the most magical Christmas of their lives. All the while, I had a secret dream that I wanted to do more for the homeless.

My dream was to 'shelter' the homeless. Early on I kept this dream pretty much to myself. We were already very busy with our core mission and sheltering the homeless seemed like a pipe dream. Yes, feeding them was important and giving them a magical Christmas every year was very special but I wanted more. When Jesus said "Feed MY Sheep," I believe he meant more than just food. I think he also meant love, caring, compassion and yes---SHELTER.

When it comes to my homeless friends I am greedy. I always want more for them. If you are homeless, getting food every day is your top priority. Next up is shelter---a safe warm place to lay your head every night. My dream was for the SoupMobile to expand beyond its feeding operation and its yearly Christmas event and now start sheltering the homeless. As time went on my dream began to take on more intensity.

In 2008 that intensity went off the charts. On October 18, 2008 Shana and I were married. We had just moved into our small 1,000 square foot cottage type home with our two dogs and two cats. And while it wasn't a big fancy type mansion it was a palace to us. We had each other, our pets and a warm safe place to lay our heads down every night. But that was a problem for me---<u>a very big problem</u>. It didn't set well with me that I got to have a safe place to bed down each night but my homeless friends did not.

For me the winter of 2008 was like the line out of the 'Charles Dickens book, A tale of Two Cities' which starts out by saying, 'It was the best of times...It was the worst of times.' That's what the winter of 2008 was like for me. Yes it was the 'best of times' as each night I got to come home to my loving wife and sleep in a warm safe bed. Yet it was the 'worst of times' as I had to do it knowing that many of our homeless family of friends weren't so lucky. It was an uneasy winter for me.

As spring arrived in 2009 I told Shana we just had to do something this year to help shelter our homeless friends. I vowed that I would not spend another winter sleeping in my own warm safe bed without doing something to shelter our homeless friends. Somehow, someway the SoupMobile would be in the sheltering business by the winter of 2009. I was committed and there was no turning back.

So having made that vow I sprang into action. I called a meeting to announce to my staff that we were going to do something to shelter the homeless by the winter of 2009. I didn't know exactly what it would be, but it would be something. I was not going to spend another winter in my home without doing something to give shelter to the ones that Jesus called the 'least of these.'

I've got to give special kudos to my staff. They knew it had been an act of madness when I started the SoupMobile in 2003 without a deep pocket donor or the support of a church. They were keenly aware what an act of lunacy it was for me to propose our Christmas event in 2005 when we had absolutely no realistic hope of pulling it off. Now I had gone off the deep end again and my staff was ready, willing and able to go out on that limb with me. All of a sudden 'I' wasn't the only one with a dream to shelter the homeless. Now the SoupTeam came on board and it became a 'we' project. WE dreamed of sheltering the homeless!

I felt like WE were on a mission---a mission from God to shelter the homeless. In Matthew 25:35 Jesus says, *"For I was hungry and you gave Me food; I was thirsty and you gave Me drink; I was a stranger and you took Me in."*

I've got to give credit to my amazing staff as they jumped right on board with me. They knew we didn't have the money to start a shelter program; they knew we didn't have the support to start such a program and they knew we already had a full plate running our regular feeding operation and putting on our Christmas event every year. Most important, they knew we had absolutely NO experience running a shelter program for the homeless. Yet they all gave the idea a thumbs up.

You see by this time they had seen how Jesus had continually parted the Red Seas for the SoupMobile. They knew that when Jesus gives you a mission, he gives you the means to do it. However we knew from past experience working with Jesus that we would have to do our part. We couldn't just sit back and twiddle our thumbs and let Jesus do all the work.

So spring into action we did. Over the spring and summer of 2009 we met with zoning officials, housing advocates, shelter administrators, builders and anyone else we felt could give us insight and guidance in sheltering the homeless. During that time we looked at over 100 homes, apartments and duplexes that could be considered possible shelter for our homeless for the coming winter. We left no stone unturned in checking out every contingency and every possibility. We finally settled on our plan to shelter the homeless starting the winter of 2009. We would call it <u>SoupMobile Village.</u>

Many shelters for the homeless are what we call a 'bed for the night.' These are shelters where you check in every night and then very early the next morning you have to leave and spend the rest of the day on the streets. I'm not knocking 'bed for a night' shelters. They are an important part of getting homeless people off the streets every night.

But in our greed for the homeless we wanted more. We wanted <u>SoupMobile Village</u> to be more than just a bed for a night. Here is how we envisioned the Village. It would be a series of group homes located all over the Dallas area. Each group home designed to take a homeless person right off the streets, put a roof over their heads, clean them up, get them a job and help them become productive members of their community. Our group homes would be 'supportive' housing which is a combination of housing and services intended as a cost-effective way to help homeless men and women lead stable, productive lives. The SoupMobile Village 'supportive' group housing would be coupled with partner programs that provided social services such as job training, life skills training, counseling services and mentorship. We envisioned going far beyond the bed for a night concept.

SoupMobile Village was now ready to leave the drawing board and become a reality. First up was our plan to open a group <u>Men's Home</u> before the winter of 2009 set in. And while we had already done our homework, the true kickoff of the drive for the <u>Men's Home</u> would take place in August of 2009.

Let me digress for a moment and talk about the month of August. It seems like every crucial moment in SoupMobile history has been in August. The SoupMobile was born in August 2003. In August 2005 I had that fateful staff meeting where I announced we would host 100 homeless people in a world class fancy hotel that very Christmas. Now in August of 2009 we would kick off the drive for a <u>Men's Home</u> in SoupMobile Village. To top it all off I was born in the month of August. I'm not sure what all this means, but as August rolls around each year my staff's eyes get just a little bit bigger and wider as they wait in anticipation to see what new mind blowing idea God has put into my head. By the way, now that you know my birthday is in August, I just want to say two words: **<u>Rolls Royce!</u>**

Okay, enough digression. Let's go back to how this chapter began with talk about a Perfect Storm. Back to the Perfect Storm that hit the SoupMan in August of 2009. Before going any further let me remind you of the definition of a Perfect Storm. <u>*A 'Perfect Storm' is an event where a rare combination of events creates a disastrous situation.*</u> Here's the scoop on the SoupMan's Perfect Storm!

Early in 2009 the <u>Main</u> Board of the SoupMobile had already agreed, that before the winter of 2009 set in, we would expand our operation to now include sheltering the homeless. In August of 2009 the SoupMobile's <u>Advisory</u> Board was scheduled to meet. The Advisory Board sits just below the SoupMobile's Main Board and its mission is to advise and assist the Main Board in completing its mission. As Executive Director of the SoupMobile I sit on the Main Board and thus I make it a point to never attend the Advisory Board meetings because I don't want to unduly influence their agenda.

And even though the Advisory Board has no formal voting power like the Main Board, its advice and counsel are still highly valued. The key topic of discussion at the fateful August 2009 meeting was to be how the Advisory Board could assist the Main Board in getting the <u>funding</u> we would need to open a Group Men's Home in SoupMobile Village before the winter of 2009 set in. At least that's what I thought their main agenda would be.

I could not have been more wrong. As I waited at home, the Advisory Board met at SoupMobile Headquarters to discuss SoupMobile Village. It was with eager anticipation that I waited to hear the results of that meeting. I was anxious to hear their ideas of how to get that first group Men's Home up and running before winter set in. I knew they would have plenty of great ideas on how to get the funding for the Men's Home. Oh was I in for a rude awakening. I got hit with the Perfect Storm. Let me explain.

At that fateful Advisory Board meeting I had multiple board members attending who had already told me that they were strongly in favor of bringing the group Men's Home on line by the winter of 2009. Several other members really liked the idea but weren't sure how we would raise the funds. One other member was neutral but had been supportive of my ideas in the past. Also attending that meeting were two brand new board members. I felt that both of them would be highly instrumental in helping us get the funding for the Men's Home. One of them was a local banker who I felt confident would have plenty of resources to either finance the home himself or certainly refer me to an agency that could provide the financing.

My other ace in the hole was the other new board member (who I will call Bert). He was well known in Dallas as being a master fundraiser. His reputation literally preceded him. His rolodex was chock full of names and numbers of wheelers and dealers in the Dallas area. I knew that a few calls from him on behalf of the SoupMobile would easily get the money flowing. So I felt like all the pieces were in place. An Advisory Board that was already generally supportive of the Men's Home; a banker with access to funding and Bert---the master fundraiser who could tap into whatever funding the banker could not.

Then the Perfect Storm hit. The Advisory Board was scheduled to meet at 10:00AM on that fateful Saturday August morning. At about 9:00AM a very heavy thunderstorm hit the Dallas area---right about the time the Board members were all driving to the meeting. My key, Number #1 Men's Home supporter was caught in a flash flood as he was driving to the meeting. While he was okay, his car was flooded and trapped in the flood waters. He never made the meeting. **Strike One!**

Another of my top supporters had been out of town and was delayed getting back in time for the meeting. **Strike Two!**

At this same meeting there was going to be a changing of the guard. The current Chairman of the Advisory Board was stepping down and the new chairman was to officially take over as soon as the August board meeting was finished. Both gentlemen had previously been supportive of the Men's Home, but each of them was restrained at the meeting because neither of them wanted to step on the other ones toes. **Strike Three!**

Things were about to get a lot worse. Bert, the master fundraiser had decided (unbeknownst to me) that he was strongly against the SoupMobile expanding its mission to include sheltering the homeless. And even though this was his first Advisory board meeting, I had been totally confident that he would be the key piece of the puzzle (along with the banker) to get the funding we needed. My oh my, how naïve I was. I found out later that Bert had spent a large part of the meeting explaining in a clear, concise and logical manner why the SoupMobile should NOT enter the Sheltering business. **Strike Four!**

Bert made some very strong arguments to the Advisory Board on why we should not push ahead with the Men's Home. He explained that the SoupMobile did not have experience in sheltering the homeless. He stressed that we did not have the financial resources to expand our operation. He carefully explained that there could be some risk in sheltering homeless people. His bottom line was that we should stick to what we did best---which was feeding the homeless. He noted that we had virtually perfected our feeding operation and we should focus on what we knew was tried and true.

Bert's convincing arguments along with the absence of two of my key supporters and the changing of the guard issue put the board in stalemate. Absolutely nothing got done. There were no ideas put forward on how to assist the Main Board in completing a mission they had already approved. Not one single idea was put on the table of how we would find the funds to purchase the Men's Home before the winter of 2009. My banker was silent and Bert was clearly <u>not</u> going to be pulling out his rolodex and calling any wheelers and dealers in town to help us get the funding.

The SoupMan had just been hit by the Perfect Storm. When I got word later that evening from the incoming Chairman of the Advisory Board about the results of the meeting I was dumbfounded. At first I thought he was joking but I quickly realized he was dead serious. I couldn't even get angry—I was too much in shock. I just never saw it coming. It never occurred to me for even one moment that the Advisory Board would be stalemated. Did I mention---I never saw it coming!

Making things worse was I was all alone that Saturday evening. My wife Shana was out of town visiting friends and she wasn't there for me to talk it out with. Shana had always been extremely supportive of the SoupMobile and was very excited about the SoupMobile Village Men's Home. So there I was—all alone and completely in shock. Our dream of having the Men's Home go online before the winter of 2009 had hit a brick wall. We were dead in the water. I just could not believe it.

As the shock wore off I started getting mad. Oh, I know what you are thinking---I must have been mad at Bert. What a monkey wrench he had thrown in our plans. Nope, it wasn't Bert I was mad at---it was God. Now don't get me wrong, I did consider taking Bert off my Christmas Card list, but clearly it was God I was most upset with. After all, he's the one running the show down here on this earth.

God and I were about to tangle. And even though I knew I was completely out of my league with HIM, I went at him head on. The first thing I said to God was, "thanks for going on Vacation today." I went on to say, don't you think you could have waited a day before you sprang a major thunderstorm on Dallas and flooded out the car of my key supporter. Couldn't you have at least waited until after the Advisory Board Meeting was over before you opened the heavens and poured out a torrent of water. Yep, no two ways about it, I was mad at God. I'd like to sugar coat it and say I was just a <u>little</u> upset or maybe say I was just a <u>little</u> distressed but truth be told, I was mad.

All alone, I paced all over the house. Remember Shana was visiting friends that weekend. I asked God---WHY? Why did you let this happen? Why did you not step in and make that Advisory Board Meeting go the way 'I' wanted? (Hmm, there's that 'I' word again). I said, don't you know it's August and winter will be upon us in a few months? I kept at God with question after question. I went on and on and didn't let up for hours. I wanted answers and I wanted them now. God responded by saying ABSOLUTELY NOTHING! It was complete utter silence. Not one word, thought or unction from him. Nothing, nada, zilch.

Well by this time I had worn myself out. I laid down on the couch and fell fast asleep. I woke up a few hours later and it was 1:00AM in the morning---Sunday morning. By then my anger had subsided, but I still wanted answers. I went back at God. Now I started trying to reason with him. I carefully explained all the reasons why a Men's Home was important. I reminded him of how faithfully we had done our homework in researching all the information about sheltering the homeless. I mentioned how we believed that 'Feeding HIS Sheep' included love, caring, compassion and SHELTER.

Once again God responded by saying ABSOLUTELY NOTHING! I started to get upset again. I needed answers from God. So I kept at him all night. I yammered on and on. Looking back I'm not sure I even stopped talking long enough to let God get a word in edgewise. Hey, what can I say, when the SoupMan goes off the deep end, he goes all the way.

By now it was almost dawn. I was tired and discouraged. In desperation I did something that I had never done before. I went over and picked up the phone and dialed: 1-800 MY GOD. Yes you heard right! I called God on the phone. It's absolutely true. Nothing else had worked. I had ranted at God; I had accused him of going on Vacation; I had asked him WHY over and over again and I had even tried to reason with him. All with absolutely no success. So at the end of my rope I picked up the phone and dialed: 1-800 MY GOD. For those of you that don't know me well, you might be thinking---'oh boy, this guy has really lost it.' But for my close friends that do know me well, they would just nonchalantly nod their heads and say, 'yeah, that sounds just like something the SoupMan would do.' Welcome to my world!!!

As I held the phone to my ear all I could hear was the dial tone. I started speaking very softly to God. I said "okay God, I've been flapping my big mouth all night---now I'm going to just shut up and listen---you've got the floor." Literally within seconds a powerful thought came to my mind. The thought said: PUT UP or SHUT UP.

I <u>hung up the phone</u> at the speed of light. I sat there in stunned silence as I absorbed what God had said to me. I knew instantly what he meant when he said 'PUT UP or SHUT UP.' God was telling ME to finance the Men's Home. He was telling ME to put up the money to buy the home. He was telling ME to Put Up the funds for the home or Shut Up.

Do you remember the 1976 movie Taxi Driver with Robert DeNiro. In the movie there is a scene in which DeNiro is looking into a mirror at himself, imagining a confrontation which would give him a chance to draw his gun. He says one of the most famous movie lines of all time, "You talkin' to me?--- You talkin' to me?--- You talkin' to me?"

Well God had just told me to Put Up or Shut Up. I became an instant twin of Robert DeNiro as I <u>picked the phone back up</u> and said back to God,

> **You talkin' to me?**
>
> **You talkin' to me?**
>
> **You talkin' to me?**

If they gave out Academy Awards for the best impersonation of an actor, I would have won hands down that morning.

I couldn't believe what God was telling me to do. He was asking me to put up the money to buy the Men's Home. No way, I didn't have that kind of money. Not a chance, it just wasn't going to happen, no-no-no! With the phone still in my hand I reminded him I did not have the money. That was a big mistake on my part because the next thought that blasted into my head was, 'Yes You Do!' And God was right--- technically I did have the money. It was in my pension plan---funds that I had set aside for retirement. I actually did have enough money to buy the Men's Home if I dipped into my retirement funds.

Still on the phone I tried to start reasoning with God again. I told God that I was not an eccentric millionaire with money to burn. I reminded him I had actually been drawing down my retirement funds from the very inception of the SoupMobile to supplement my poverty level wages. I even got out a pen, paper and calculator and showed God how my average yearly pay was less than $13,000 per year for the first seven years I worked as Executive Director for the SoupMobile.

I reiterated that because the SoupMobile had always operated on a shoestring, I had to dip into my retirement funds each and every year just to pay my own personal bills. I ended by explaining that I had already dipped heavily into my retirement savings and now going back and withdrawing what little was left to purchase the Men's Home just wasn't fair.

In my agitated state of mind, I felt I was very convincing in my arguments and that my reasoning with God was 100% correct. But there was one small problem---God didn't seem much impressed. Back came that powerful thought in my head---PUT UP or SHUT UP.

Okay, that was it---I knew when I was licked. I gently hung up the phone, got down on my knees, bowed my head and very quietly said, "Thy Will Be Done." It had taken me all of Saturday evening and all through the night and into the next morning before I finally surrendered to God's 'Will.' That night I was a slow learner!

A couple of things really struck me about that night. Even though I raged at God, accused him of going on Vacation, yammered on and on, fought against his will and took like what seemed forever to come around to his way of thinking---he never got mad at me, never had one cross word with me, never sent any lightning bolts my way, stayed incredibly patient with me and most important HE never stopped loving me. No matter how much I got off track, he just kept on loving me. Is God fabulous or what!

Okay, so now I can hear you saying, 'Hey SoupMan, don't keep us in suspense, what happened with

SoupMobile Village?' Did you get the Men's Home up and running before the winter of 2009 hit???

Well, just turn the page to the next chapter for your answer!

Chapter 5
<u>After</u> the Perfect Storm!

If you want to see the sunshine, you have to weather the storm.

Frank Lane

So having weathered the Perfect Storm and finally submitting to God's will, I did exactly what he told me to do. He said PUT UP or SHUT UP and I PUT UP. I dipped into my dwindling retirement fund and put up the money to fund the Men's Home in SoupMobile Village.

However it's important that you know that I did ask God for a little bit of relief on this point. I asked him if it would be okay for me to loan the money to the SoupMobile and have it paid back to me later, so I could put the money back in my retirement fund. But this time when I asked, I made no demands, didn't yammer on and on and did not accuse him of going on Vacation. I asked softly and quietly and waited for his answer. I can truthfully say I did not hear him answer in an audible voice and I really didn't have a powerful thought or answer come into my head. What I did have was an incredible sense of peace about my request. The Bible talks about the 'peace of God that passes all understanding.' I think the peace I felt at that moment was God's way of saying okay. I needed him to cut me some slack and he did.

But before you think I took the easy way out, let me point out that making a loan of this magnitude to the SoupMobile was not without risk. The SoupMobile operates on a shoestring. We watch our pennies and are mission oriented---not salary/perks oriented. There was no guarantee the SoupMobile would even be able to pay me back. Now if we had been some big charity like the Red Cross or Salvation Army, loaning the money would have been no big deal as they could clearly pay it back. With the baby SoupMobile there were no such guarantees. But that didn't matter---God told me to PUT UP and I did. How it all came out in the wash was up to him.

So now we had the funding to purchase our Men's Home. Winter was just a few months away and time was tight. We had already done our homework and we knew what properties were available in our price range. We made an offer on a middle class townhome in a nice middle class neighborhood. Nothing super fancy but certainly a very workable home for our homeless men. After a quick negotiation with the seller we came to a fair price and the deal was done. The home needed some tender loving care and I put out an appeal to my supporters for help in doing a quick update and remodeling job. I got an overwhelming response of help and within a short period of time we were set for the Grand Opening of the Men's Home which took place on October 7, 2009.

Oh how sweet it was! We had met our deadline and the Men's Home was opened just before the winter of 2009 came upon us. I can't tell you the joy that just filled my heart. Now I could sleep in my own warm, safe bed knowing that we had gotten SoupMobile Village up and running. It seems God must have also been pretty happy because we soon found out he had even grander plans for SoupMobile Village. Here's the lowdown. Listen up because this story will knock your socks off!

At the Grand Opening of the Men's Home in October of 2009 we were blessed with major news coverage. One of the local Dallas TV stations came out and did a story on the opening and the Dallas Morning News ran a 'front page' full length story. We thought this was all very nice but we had no idea of what that news coverage would lead to. We were about to watch God move in a powerful way.

A local couple from Coppell, Texas (Roger & Joy) had seen the TV coverage and read the front page story in the newspaper. It seems our story tapped deep into their own desire to help the homeless. Up until the news coverage they had never heard of the SoupMobile and we didn't have a clue of who they were. God was about to play the middleman and bring us together.

Shortly after the Grand Opening of the Men's Home I got a call from Joy. She asked if she could come and volunteer with us and also chat with me. We love to get good volunteers so I invited her to come and serve food to the homeless with us. I really didn't know what was on her mind. She did come, did serve and then we did chat. She had a lot of questions about the Men's Home and our future plans for SoupMobile Village. I explained to Joy that we envisioned a series of Group Homes located all over the Dallas area. Each group home specifically designed to take a homeless person off the streets, put a roof over their heads, clean them up, get them a job and help them become productive members of the community. Joy thanked me for my time and asked if she could come back and serve with us a different time. I said yes and that was the end of it--- or so I thought.

A few weeks later she did come back and served with us and once again asked to chat with me. She had even more questions about SoupMobile Village. I diligently answered them, she thanked me and asked if she and her husband could come and serve with us AND chat! Ah, as Sherlock Holmes would say, 'the plot thickens.' I still wasn't totally sure where this was all going but clearly they were checking us out. Sure enough a few weeks later both Joy and Roger showed up, served with us and then asked to chat. Well by this time the questions about the future of the Village got pretty detailed. I knew they weren't here to have tea and crumpets.

They asked if they could go by the TownHome complex where the Men's Home was located and walk the grounds to get a feel for the area. I said yes and gave them the complex address. Then they asked if I could arrange for them to tour the inside of the Men's Home and meet some of the residents. I said yes and a few days later they were in the home and talking with the men who lived there. By this time they had expressed to me an interest in possibly sponsoring another home in SoupMobile Village. They made no promises, but told me they would be in prayer about it. They did ask me this question---'IF they did decide to sponsor the next home, would we be willing to designate it to be a Women's Home?' Well this was an easy question for me to answer because we had already planned that whenever the next group home went on line, it would be a Women's Home. Like any big city, Dallas has both homeless men and women.

Well, that was the last I heard from Roger & Joy for a while. Christmas was fast approaching and we were in full bore planning for our year end Christmas event in which we put 500 homeless people up at the downtown Dallas Hyatt Regency Hotel and give them the most magical Christmas of their lives. Then a few weeks before Christmas I got an early Christmas present. Roger and Joy told me they would sponsor the full purchase price of the next home in SoupMobile Village---the Women's Home. Oh glory be to God. Just four months earlier in August of 2009 the plans for SoupMobile Village had been hit by the Perfect Storm and the Men's Home project was dead in the water. Now just a few short months later, not only did we have the Men's Home on line but now we had the cash for the Women's Home. Does God move fast or what!

I thanked Roger and Joy for their gift and as I drove home that night in my 2002 Chrysler PT Cruiser (yes, for all you readers of my 1st book, I still have the car), I decided to pull off the road and have a chat with God. I pulled out my cell phone and dialed 1-800 MY GOD. I have to admit I was chuckling as I did it and I think God was laughing too. I said, "God, it looks to me like you allowed that Perfect Storm in my life so that I would have to PUT UP and then you rewarded my faith by getting us the funding for the second home in record time." I didn't even need for God to answer. I knew he had tested me just as he had tested many in the Bible. And just like in the Bible he rewarded my faith.

Over the years it seems like God and I have reached a kind of gentlemen's agreement. He requires me to <u>first</u> go out on the limb---in faith and then he rides to my rescue. That's what he did when we started the SoupMobile in 2003. He didn't give us the money and the means in advance. He made us start the SoupMobile with absolutely nothing and then he came and worked miracles to reward that faith. The same thing happened again in 2005 when we started our Christmas Event called <u>Celebrate Jesus.</u> We didn't have the money for it, the support, the expertise or even a hotel to host the event. But in faith we went out on a limb and said we were going to do it and sure enough God rewarded that faith by pulling off a major miracle in getting us the Hyatt Regency to host the event. (You'll have to read my first book to get more details on that miracle).

Well you might think that this is the end of the story but it's not. God had another ace up his sleeve when it came to SoupMobile Village. Using the funds from Roger & Joy, we did purchase the Women's Home in early spring 2010. It needed a lot of fixing up but Roger & Joy mobilized their friends and church members to ride to our rescue. It turned out Joy was pretty good at home decorating and Roger can swing a mean hammer! They didn't just put up the funding for the home, they put their heart and soul into the Women's Home.

The Grand Opening of the Women's Home was set for April 1, 2010. We had a big ribbon cutting ceremony planned, a lot of invited guests, news coverage from a local TV station, a reporter from National Public Radio and we even got a mention in the Dallas Morning News. In the audience at the ribbon cutting ceremony was a local couple from

Plano, Texas,(Rick & Linda). Rick asked if he could say a few words before we actually cut the ribbon. The gist of his speech was that he and Linda felt called by the Lord to sponsor the next home in SoupMobile Village. Oh my, you could have knocked me over with a feather! We hadn't even cut the ribbon yet on the Women's Home and Rick was handing me a check to complete the funding for the next home. Did I mention that God moves fast!

Three months later on July 9, 2010 we officially opened the 'Family Home' in SoupMobile Village. For those of you who are keeping up, that's three Group Homes in less than a year. Didn't I tell you that this story would knock your socks off!!! We truly can 'do all things through Christ.'

I know some of you are wondering about Bert. You know, my Advisory Board member that came out strongly against SoupMobile Village. Well, you will be happy to know that I did <u>not</u> take Bert off my Christmas Card list. Yes, I admit I thought about it but I had made my piece with God and that was enough for me.

I'm pleased to tell you that Bert and I are still friends and even though he no longer serves on the Advisory Board he routinely steers help my way. We respect and value each other and both of us have a passion for reaching out to the ones Jesus calls the 'least of these.' So let's take a moment and talk about Bert's actions at that fateful Advisory Board meeting. Bert was dead set against the SoupMobile expanding its operation to include sheltering the homeless. He made some very convincing arguments about why we should NOT get into the sheltering business. He had lobbied the board telling them we didn't have any experience in the sheltering business; how we did not have the financial resources to shelter the homeless and he noted that it could be risky sheltering homeless people. He finished by saying we should stick to what we knew best, which was 'feeding' the homeless.

Guess what? Bert was absolutely 100% correct. Everything he said was true. We didn't have the money or expertise and it was risky. So we had to make a decision. Did we go with Bert's sage advice or did we hearken to that guy from 2,000 years ago who said "Feed MY Sheep." As I said earlier in this book, we think that Jesus meant more than just food when he said "Feed My Sheep." We believe that he also meant love, caring, compassion and yes--- Shelter!

Now for a moment let me put the 'I' word back in this shelter story. Remember I'm not crazy about the 'I' word, but I think you need to hear more on how I personally feel about sheltering the homeless. Jesus talks about 'Feeding <u>HIS</u> Sheep.' But I'm like a mother hen and I think of the homeless as <u>my</u> sheep to. It absolutely saddens me when I think of the multitude of homeless that go without shelter every night. These homeless people are my friends, they are my people and they are my family. We are all one in the Lord. The question of the SoupMobile getting into the sheltering business was not so much of a practical decision for me---it was more of a 'heart' decision. My heart longs to do more for the homeless than just feed them.

In the Bible in Matthew 25:45, it says, *'Then shall HE answer them, saying---verily I say unto you, inasmuch as ye did it **<u>not</u>** to one of the least of these, ye did it **<u>not</u>** to Me.'* So let's lay it all on the line. If you knew that the homeless person standing on the corner was Jesus---wouldn't you move heaven and earth to shelter him? Of course you would. If you knew it was Jesus, you would shelter him in your own home. Well, there are thousands of homeless men and women out there. One of them just may be Jesus.

So it was my heart that drove my decision to start SoupMobile Village. What Bert didn't know, was that I had a gentlemen's agreement with God that said I had to step out in faith first and then let God reward that faith. If I had not taken the money out of my retirement fund and financed that first group home, Roger & Joy would have never showed up on our radar and there would have been no second home. And if there had been no second home, Rick & Linda would not have attended the Grand Opening of that 2nd home, and there would have been no 3rd home.

So the bottom line is that Bert was technically correct in his assessment. And for 99% of the charities out there, his advice <u>not</u> to go into the sheltering business may have been spot on. But for that 1% of the charities that have a gentlemen's agreement with God, it's all about crawling out on that limb and letting God do his thing. Feeding HIS Sheep is NOT about following Conventional Wisdom, it's about following Jesus. If we had followed conventional wisdom there would be no SoupMobile, no SoupMobile Christmas Event called <u>Celebrate Jesus</u> and no SoupMobile Village.

When Jesus said "Feed MY Sheep," it **<u>wasn't a suggestion</u>**. It was a call to action! I am reminded of a quote by Betty Eadie, "Faith is not complacent; faith is action. You don't have faith and wait. When you have faith you move."

So it seems that God and I have this gentlemen's agreement when it comes to the growth of the SoupMobile. He requires me to work without a net-- at least a visible net. I have to move first (in faith) and then he rewards that faith. I admit things can get pretty dicey sometimes as I crawl out on that limb, but if you look real close you will see Jesus already out there waiting.

In August of 2009 I was hit by the Perfect Storm:

It was <u>God's</u> Perfect Storm!

Chapter 6
Take a Vacation Dude!

A vacation is what you take when you can no longer take what you've been taking.

    Earl Wilson---syndicated columnist

By now you know I have written two books. Both of them have the word Vacation in their title. Both books are all about the miracles of the Lord!

The 1st book is titled: **<u>Is</u> God On Vacation?**

The 2nd book is titled: **God Is <u>NOT</u> On Vacation!**

Recently the concept of a Vacation came up in a different kind of way. One day we had a group of young volunteers at the SoupMobile that had come to help us serve food to the homeless. I always try to spend some time with our volunteers before we actually go out and feed the homeless. It's a chance to get to know them better, answer any questions they might have and brief them on what we will be doing for the day.

Somehow during that chat session the conversation got around to vacations. One of the youngsters then asked me when was the last time I had gone on a vacation? I hesitated because I could not readily remember the last time I had been on a vacation. I replied that it had been years since I had been on a real vacation. Then another member of the youth group blurted out, "Take a Vacation Dude."

Without missing a beat, I replied, "I am on Vacation Dude." That little episode got me to be thinking about personal vacations. It occurred to me that over the years many people had said to me at one time or another, 'hey SoupMan, why don't you take a vacation?' And until that youngster blurted out, "Take a Vacation Dude," I had always kind of sloughed it off and never given it much thought.

It's not that I'm against vacations or opposed to going on a vacation. It's more that I believe I'm already on vacation. Many think of a vacation as a time to get away from work and go and recharge their batteries. But I don't need to go off to some exotic port to do that. I recharge my batteries every day as the SoupMan. I'm kind of like the battery in the car you drive every day. If you don't drive the car, your battery will get weaker and weaker and eventually go dead. It's the very act of driving the car and letting your alternator charge the car battery that makes it all work. The more you drive the car the more the battery gets recharged.

I'm just like the car. I live, eat and breathe the SoupMobile 24 hours per day, seven days a week and 12 months a year. I never get burned out, never feel depressed and never feel the need to get away from it all. You see, I've never considered what I do as work. If it is work, I never got that memo. It's even hard to refer to it as a labor of love, because I don't consider it labor. It's not that I work 24 hours per day. It's more that I <u>live</u> the SoupMobile 24 hours per day.

It's actually three powerful words---'Feed My Sheep'---that drive me every single day of my life. When I awake in the morning those are the first words I think of. And when I go to sleep each night they are the last three words on my mind.

Feeding HIS Sheep is not work, it's a joy. I don't **have** to feed and shelter the homeless---I **get** to feed and shelter them. I don't **have** to go to work every day---I **get** to go to the candy store every day. So just like your car alternator recharges your car battery the more you drive, the more I live, eat and breathe being the SoupMan---the more the love of Jesus recharges my batteries.

Jesus said "Feed MY Sheep." I think somehow people get it in their heads that this has to be a difficult, energy draining and laborious job. It's not! In reality it's a total joy. Does the job require effort, energy, skill, purpose and elbow grease? Yes, absolutely it does! Do problems and issues come up that require creative thinking and about of the box solutions? Again, absolutely yes! But when Jesus gives you a call to action, I believe you will experience 'joy' as you do HIS bidding. I am living proof of this.

We've all heard of the Monday blues. Yep, the day we have to get up and go back to work. I never get the Monday blues, Tuesday blues, Wednesday blues, Thursday blues, Friday blues, Saturday blues or Sunday Blues. Every day for me is a joy. For me, being the Executive Director of the SoupMobile is not work---it's a vacation. Yes a daily vacation.

I don't need to get away from work to recharge my batteries because I don't consider what I do as work. Feeding HIS Sheep work??? I don't think so! Feeding HIS Sheep is total unbridled JOY! In John 15, Jesus says, *"These things have I spoken unto you, that my joy might remain in you, and that your joy might be full."*

Having said all of the above I do think it is important to go on vacations. And I include myself in that assessment. Yes, the SoupMan needs to go on vacation sometimes. In fact as I write this chapter, I see that the SoupGirl is looking over my shoulder and nodding in the affirmative about how very important vacations are.

It's not that I'm opposed to going on a vacation. I'm not! It's not that I won't ever go on vacation. I will. It's just that I don't need to go on vacation to get away from work to recharge my batteries. When I go on a vacation it will be for other reasons--- like meeting new people, seeing grand sights, visiting family, eating new kinds of food and experiencing new things.

What it won't be is to recharge my batteries. I do that every day as I go about 'Feeding HIS Sheep.'

Think about it---what could be more rewarding, more fulfilling, more joyous than doing something that Jesus has called us to do.

So in answer to my young friend who said "Take a Vacation Dude," I can only reply:

I am on Vacation Dude!!!

Chapter 7
The Great Divide!

I am not sure exactly what heaven will be like, but I know that when we die and it comes time for God to judge us, he will not ask, 'How many good things have you done in your life?' Rather he will ask, 'How much <u>LOVE</u> did you put into what you did?'

Mother Teresa

I'm often asked what it's like dealing with the homeless. Is it easy or is it hard? Is it sugar & spice or is it trouble & turmoil? Is it calm seas & smooth sailing or is it troubled waters & dark skies.

The answer is YES! It's all of the above. The homeless have a unique set of issues that requires a unique set of solutions. Dealing with the homeless takes a different kind of mind set. Working with the homeless is NOT for the meek, but you must have meekness in you to do it.

Whether you are a paid service provider or a volunteer---most people start working in the homeless sector with great intentions, open hearts and a gung ho attitude of making a real difference in the lives of the ones Jesus calls the 'least of these.'

After many years of working in our business (helping the homeless) I've noticed a strange phenomenon. Some people start to have a change of heart after working with the homeless for an extended period of time. After a while those great intentions, open hearts and gung ho attitudes start to change. Their hearts harden and an adversarial relationship develops between the service providers and the homeless they serve. It becomes an US against THEM mentality.

Before going any further let me stress that this phenomenon is NOT true of everyone working with the homeless. However I've seen enough of this hardening of hearts to know it's true of some of them. A labor of love changes to 'it's a labor.' The love falls by the wayside and all that is left is that it's just a job. It's at that point that The Great Divide starts to appear. It's at that point that the relationship becomes adversarial. It's at that point that it becomes US against THEM.

Why? What happens to create this Great Divide between the providers and the homeless they are supposed to be serving. It's actually a series of things. Sometimes it's because their 'bubble is burst.' The providers start with a Pollyanna view of dealing with the homeless. They think it's going to be all sugar and spice and when they find out it's not, the bubble breaks. Here's what I tell my staff---if you are going to deal with people (the homeless) that are down in the mud, be prepared to get muddy yourself. Think of a world class surgeon that has to operate on a patient. It's going to get messy and bloody. And even though the final result of the surgery is usually positive, getting to that final result can be a rough road.

Dealing with the homeless is much the same as the work of the world class surgeon. It won't be all peaches and cream. Sometimes we are going to get very muddy reaching into the world of the homeless. Sometimes the homeless do things that seem improper. And when they do those wrongful things, some (not all) service providers get upset. Let me give you an example.

There is a lady in Dallas that used to feed the homeless. Let's call her Nan. Every Sunday Nan would rush home after church and cook up 100 hot, delicious dinners with all the fixings. Using her own money she would prepare 100 heaping plates of food and drive into downtown Dallas and set up at one location and serve the homeless people in her feeding line. Her meals were top of the line. Each of the 100 plates was overflowing with meat, potatoes, vegetables and dinner rolls. Each person in line was supposed to receive one of those 100 plates.

But there was a problem---a very serious problem. Each time she would pull up to the feeding location there would usually be about 200 homeless people waiting and there would be a mad rush from the homeless to get the food from her. They would push and shove to get to the front of the line, sometimes there would be fights and generally it was a disorderly situation.

Nan used to complain to me about how the homeless acted in her feeding line. Many times she would call me and rant about the homeless that she was feeding. She called them ungrateful and ill behaved. She was highly offended that 'she' was taking her Sunday to prepare all this food and the homeless were not acting the way she thought they should. On the surface Nan seemed to have a point. Here she was working on a Sunday to provide this wonderful food and the homeless were acting unruly. Nan looked to be in the right and the homeless who pushed and shoved in her line looked like the ungrateful ones. However, looks can sometimes be deceiving.

It seems that her heart had become hardened against those she served. Instead of looking for solutions, Nan was spending too much time blaming the homeless. Yes, she clearly had a problem with her feeding line. Each time she fed on Sunday there would be about 200 homeless people waiting for her. These were hungry people. Men, women and sometimes even children. They knew she was only bringing food for 100 of them.

What would you do if you were one of the hungry homeless people waiting to get fed? What would you do if you were a single mother in that line with your children? What would you do if you were an elderly homeless man who hadn't eaten all day? What would you do if you were just an average homeless person that needed food? You would also be pushing and shoving to get to the front of the line. Hunger drives people to do things they would not normally do in so call 'genteel' society.

I finally decided that I would try to give Nan a different take on the situation. I told her that the homeless that were pushing and shoving, fighting and struggling to get to the front of the line were NOT at fault. I told her that she was the one causing the problem. I explained that she was the one creating the turmoil by bringing 100 meals when she knew there would be 200 people in the line. I told her that if she was one of the 200 people in line she would be acting the same way. She was horrified and got highly offended. She said "how dare I fault her when she was taking her valuable time and using her own money to prepare these wonderful meals." I told her that while what she was doing in preparing the meals was commendable, her execution needed tweaking.

I tried to explain to Nan, that as the providers of the food---it was our job to figure out ways to make it all work. With an attitude of defiance she asked me what I thought she should do. First I asked if it was possible for her to bring more meals to serve. She said she could not afford to purchase the food for 200 meals. That made sense to me. I could completely understand if she didn't have the money to purchase more food. Then I suggested a second solution. I said if you can't afford to buy food for 200 meals why don't you divide the 100 meals in half and make them into 200 meals. I reminded her that the 100 plates she was already bringing were overflowing with food and that even though the meal for each person would be smaller, that each person would still get plenty. By doing this there would be no reason for anyone in the line to push and shove---they would all know they would get fed. Nan strongly objected to this solution. She went back to her mantra of how she put in a lot of time, money and effort to cook the 100 meals. She said the homeless should be grateful and stop acting unruly.

Do you see what happened? It became all about Nan. How terrific she was to buy and prepare these meals and how she gave of her precious time each Sunday. It was all about Nan. Somehow over time Nan's heart had hardened and it became all about her---The Great Divide!

Let's get one thing straight. Nan is to be commended for buying and cooking the food each Sunday. That's an admirable thing to do. Unfortunately that's not enough. This isn't about me being right and Nan being wrong. However it is about doing the 'right' thing. It's about finding solutions for homeless problems. It's about using our imagination and bringing our own creativity to the table. We can't look to the homeless to solve all the problems. They are already down and out and it's all they can do just to survive out on the streets. As the providers we must be the ones to find ways to make it all work.

You might think Nan's story is unusual, but I see this kind of thinking all too often. I recently attended a Homeless Support Meeting. This was a meeting where homeless people could attend and express to the group their wants, needs and concerns. Usually attending those meetings would be some of the local service providers that could provide advice and assistance to the homeless that were attending. At one of those meetings a homeless gentleman was complaining how hard it was to get services.

One of the service providers was called upon to get up and give this man some advice on how to remedy his problem. Let's call her Suzzy Lou---this was a lady who had worked for many years in a <u>paid</u> position in a local agency that specialized in helping the homeless. She got up and started telling the man how he should get in line earlier in the morning so that he would have a better chance of getting help. She then gave him a few other tips on obtaining the services he needed. So far so good, but as Suzzy Lou went on, the tenor of her speech changed.

She started chastising the homeless in the room for being lazy. She repeatedly reminded them that they were getting services for free. She didn't go as far as saying they were worthless but she was heading in that direction. Then she started complaining that in the agency she worked at, the homeless got free services but that she had to pay for those same services for herself and her family. Now we were getting to the nub of Suzzy Lou's problem. She was bitter. She had worked with the homeless for years and it bothered her that they got services for free and she had to pay. She had become bitter towards the very ones she was serving. And by the way, remember she was getting paid to do her work. Somehow over the years her heart had hardened and she had become bitter towards the very ones she served---The Great Divide!

Routinely I hear service providers for the homeless complaining about how the homeless act. For example they complain that some homeless people drink alcohol to excess. It's an attitude of 'how dare they drink' when we are trying to help them. But how about we look at the situation from the perspective of the homeless person. Do some of them drink too much? Yes, they do! But think about it, if you were homeless, desperate and without hope---might you also drink to help numb the pain? Do some regular people from 'genteel' society drink too much? Well sure they do! Hey, just check out any fancy upscale bar in town at happy hour every day and you will see some people from 'genteel' society drinking to excess. We are so quick to point the finger that we forget that we are sometimes just as guilty. The Great Divide!

I also hear complaints that some homeless people do drugs. Well duh! Welcome to the real world. Drugs cross all strata of society. Rich, poor, middle class and homeless--- drugs are everywhere. It seems like almost daily we hear about some Hollywood movie star getting caught with drugs. Recently one of them got stopped because of erratic driving and the police found cocaine in her car. She claimed that she thought it was gum. Do some of the homeless do drugs. Yes, they do! And just like in regular 'genteel' society, some do it to numb the pain. The Great Divide!

Let's set the record straight right now on whether there are bad homeless people. Yes, of course there are. In every barrel there are a few bad apples. Just look across all levels of society. From the very richest to the very poorest there are some bad apples. People from all walks of life use drugs, overdo it on alcohol and break the rules. I walk in both worlds and I don't think the percentage of wrong doers in the homeless population is much different than in the regular world. The problem is that when homeless people do it we tend to be very judgmental and unforgiving. When regular people do improper things we are quicker to forgive and forget. And when movie stars do bad things we just shrug it off and buy more movie tickets.

Okay, so now I hear you asking, 'hey SoupMan---what's the solution to this Great Divide?' What do we do about this adversarial relationship that builds up between the service providers and the homeless they serve? How do we prevent this US against THEM problem?

I can give you the answer in one word: JESUS. Yes, Jesus. No, I don't mean we just go around with our hands in prayer saying Jesus, oh Jesus. What I mean is that we turn to the words of the Bible for our answer. Let's look at the words in Galatians 3:28: *"There is neither Jew nor Greek, there is neither slave nor free man, there is neither male nor female; for you are all <u>one</u> in Christ Jesus."* We need to stop thinking of ourselves as different from the homeless; as better than they are; as more righteous and stop acting like we are doing them a favor.

You've all heard the saying, 'There but for the grace of God go I.' At the SoupMobile we have changed that phrase---when we are referring to the homeless to, 'There go I.' In other words we are no better than the homeless. We are all one! We are all one in Jesus! Our circumstances may be different right now---maybe we have a house and they don't; we have a job and they don't; we have plenty of food and they don't; but we are not better than they are. We have to start thinking of the homeless as our friends, our people and our family. We have to start thinking that one of them may be Jesus in disguise. We have to treat them just like we would treat Jesus---with love, kindness, caring and compassion.

Another thing we can do to prevent The Great Divide is to change what we call the homeless. We live in a world where it seems especially important to be 'politically correct' so as not to offend anybody. Many homeless agencies call the homeless they serve their 'clients.'

Clients??? That's a term that has always puzzled me. I guess if we look at it logically, the homeless we serve are our clients. Just like in a hospital where people being treated are called patients. So I think it's okay to call them clients as long as we don't think of them as clients. We need to think of them as people, not as a number in our computers or a name on our check list. These are real live human beings. Real people with real problems, that need our help and our love.

So okay, call them clients if you must, but think of them as people---precious children of the Lord most high. Let's think of them as our friends and family. After all, we are all <u>one</u> in the family of God.

Our relationship with the homeless all starts with how we perceive them. If we view them as clients, then that's how we will treat them. But if we view them as friends and family, we will treat them in a whole different way---a better and more loving way. If we think of them as clients I believe we may set the tone for an impersonal relationship. A relationship that could lead to a hardening of our hearts as time goes by. But if we start the relationship by opening our own hearts and calling them friends and family, I believe that approach can help prevent The Great Divide.

Another way we service providers can make sure our relationship with the homeless doesn't become adversarial is to change the order of how we approach our mission of helping the homeless. Each day volunteers come to the SoupMobile to help us serve food to the homeless. Before going to serve the food I give them all a briefing on what to expect. I tell them we have two missions for the day. I start out by saying that feeding the homeless is our secondary mission---it's our number #2 mission. I go on to explain that our number ONE mission is bringing Love to the homeless people we serve. I tell them that when Jesus said "Feed MY Sheep" we believe he meant more than just food. He also meant love, caring, compassion and shelter. I finish the briefing by saying that the food is *souper* important, but that the love is number one on our agenda.

This concept of Love first may be a little unusual in some circles. Service providers are paid to serve the homeless---they aren't paid to love them. Loving them certainly isn't in their training manual. But once again I ask everyone to consider---what would Jesus do? Would he lead with Love? I'm absolutely sure he would.

So how do we prevent The Great Divide? We change our priorities. We don't think of ourselves as better or different from the homeless. We stop thinking of them as clients. We start looking at them as friends and family. Most important we change the order of our mission and bring them the Love of Jesus <u>first</u> and then bring them the services they need <u>second</u>.

One final note on The Great Divide. If you are serving the homeless either as a volunteer like Nan who cooked the 100 meals each Sunday, or a paid service provider like Suzzy Lou who has worked in a homeless agency for many years---if your heart has hardened, let me kindly and gently suggest that maybe it's time for you to do something else. Either soften your heart or think about another profession.

I'm not suggesting we let homeless people run wild and do whatever they please. Sometimes homeless people need 'tough' love, but love is the key. If you can't or won't give that love---serving the homeless may not be the best place for you to be.

There is a line in the GodFather movie that says, 'this is the business we have chosen.' Each one of us that serves the homeless has 'chosen' to do so. Nobody made us do it, it was our choice. So let's stop complaining about how the homeless act like homeless people do and let's start looking for solutions. Like maybe dividing 100 meals into 200 meals. Some other solutions when dealing with the homeless will not be so easy. Nonetheless, as the ones that serve the homeless, the mantle is on us to be creative, innovative and think out of the box.

Let's stop blaming the homeless for being homeless and let's look deep within ourselves to find solutions.

Most important let's <u>lead with love</u>. I am reminded of the Bible verse in 1Corinthians 13:1 *"If I speak in the tongues of men and angels, but have <u>not love,</u> I am only a resounding gong or clanging cymbal. If I have the gift of prophecy and can fathom all mysteries and all knowledge, and if I have a faith that can move mountains, but have <u>not love</u>, I am nothing. If I give all I possess to the poor and surrender my body to the flames, but have <u>not love</u>, I gain nothing."*

It's not enough that we just provide services to the homeless. It's not enough that we go home at night and tell our family and friends how many meals we served. It's not enough that we feed and shelter the homeless. If the love is not there, it's all for nothing.

I started this Chapter with the words of Mother Teresa and I will finish with them. She said, "It's not how much we give but how much **love** we put into the giving."

Chapter 8
Moments that Touched My Heart!

Some people wait a lifetime for a moment like this.

> Kelly Clarkson---singer, American Idol Winner

Since the birth of the SoupMobile in August of 2003, God has blessed my life with some very special moments. Moments that touched my heart. I'd like to share a few of them with you. These moments are in no particular order.

April 2005: I answered the phone at the SoupMobile. It was a young lady by the name of Shana who wanted to volunteer and had read about the SoupMobile in the newspaper. She said, "are you that SoupMan guy they wrote about in the paper?" I said yes and 3 ½ years later I married that young lady!

Christmas Eve 2009: It's three o'clock in the morning and we have 500 homeless people bedded down for the night at the Dallas Hyatt Regency Hotel. A freezing rain had been coming down all evening and the roads are virtually impassable. One of our homeless guests gets sick and needs a prescription filled immediately. Rick--one of my volunteers that night said, "I'll handle it" and somehow he did!

February 2010: A homeless man by the name of Carl reads my first book titled: Is God on Vacation? He calls my office and leaves a message saying, "I just read your book---I realized that I have not in the past been eager to read the Bible, but now I will take the time."

September 2003: The Mayor of Boxville looks out for my best interests and puts the word out on the streets, "You mess with the SoupMan and you are messing with me." (Read Chapter 9 for more details on this one).

June 2007: We are serving food to the homeless on an uncovered parking lot. The sky's open up and the rain comes down in buckets. It's a literal torrent of water. <u>Not</u> one homeless person gets out of line---they are hungry. <u>Not</u> one of my volunteers flinches and heads for cover. Rusty--one of the volunteers that day, looks up and says, "What rain—you call this rain," as the food was practically floating away.

December 2003: I had just finished serving the lunch time meal to my homeless friends and one of the homeless men came back up to me. He thanked me for the food and said he wanted to make a donation to the SoupMobile. He dug into the pocket of his threadbare blue jeans and pulled out all the money he had. It was <u>Nine Cents</u>. It was the best donation I ever received.

January 2007: Shana & I deliver a care basket of food to Jackie—a lady who had terminal cancer and only months to live. After we helped Jackie put away all the food, I ask her if Shana and I can pray for her before we leave. She says <u>NO</u>, I want to pray for you. We all join hands and Jackie proceeds to pray for Shana and myself and the SoupMobile. Wow, talk about an unselfish act. We prayed for Jackie in the car after we left. Oh boy, did we pray!

December 2008: I am counting on a donation of 500 bibles that will be used as gifts for our homeless guests at the Hyatt for Christmas. The donation falls through 10 days before Christmas. I call several churches in town to try to get them replaced but no one can help me. I pray about it and a thought comes to my mind to call Rev. Tim---the amazing Reverend that married me & Shana. I call and tell him my problem. He says, "I don't know how I will get you the Bibles, but in faith I will." Somehow, with one day to spare before Christmas--- he gets them!

Winter 2007: On two separate occasions I sleep overnight on the streets of Dallas with my homeless friends. It was cold, dark and just a little scary. My compassion for the homeless that have to sleep out there every night went up exponentially after that.

October 2008: One year **BEFORE** the SoupMobile starts housing the homeless, I change the wording on my business cards from 'Feeding the Homeless' to 'Feeding and _Housing_ the Homeless.' A step of faith based on the words of Romans 4:17 *"calleth those things which be not as though they were."*

May 2003: Three months **BEFORE** the birth of the SoupMobile, I purchase personalized license plates for my car that say SoupMan. (See Romans 4:17)

Date: Sometime soon! This moment hasn't happened yet, but it will. SoupMobile Diner opens. A restaurant that serves great food, employs homeless people and trains them to work in the restaurant industry. (Once again---See Romans 4:17)

August 2009: The SoupMobile Village Men's Home is dead in the water and it looks like there is NO chance it will go online before winter. My good friend Lon says, "David, I'm with you no matter what---if we have to set up a tent city for the homeless on my property in the country, we will do it." It never came to that---but if it had, Lon would have kept his word. That's the kind of guy he is!

November 2005: I come into work one day and my secretary says, "you know David---Shana really likes you." Naively I answer, "oh I like her too---she's a great volunteer." My secretary said, "No, you don't understand---she **REALLY** likes you." I had been totally clueless. Typical man, huh!

December 2008: I'm at Sam's buying supplies for the SoupMobile. As I am leaving I spot a gentleman who has a little booth <u>inside</u> the store. Everyone seems to be ignoring him and rushing by. I stop and ask him what he is doing there. He says he is asking for donations to buy Christmas Gifts for children whose military parents are serving in Iraq. My heart melts and I reach into my pocket and pull out all the money I have left. It's $17.00. I give it all to him---apologize that I only have $17.00 to give and leave the store. I am not two steps out of the store when I feel a tap on my shoulder. It's a woman who says, "I saw what you did back there"---she hands me a Twenty Dollar bill. God moves fast!

January 2007: It's bitterly cold and I watch with pride as one of my volunteers takes off his warm coat and gives it to a homeless man who had no coat.

Christmas 2009: One of the homeless women staying at the Hyatt for our Christmas Event gives me a big hug and thanks me for the best Christmas she ever had. As I hug her back I say "thank you for the best Christmas <u>I've</u> ever had."

April 2003: I tell my good friend Sheryl about my idea for starting up a mobile soup kitchen called the SoupMobile. Without missing a beat, she points her finger at me and says, "then you will be the SoupMan." Her prophetic words came true & then some!

October 18, 2008: Shana says, **"I Do."** I become the most blessed man on the planet!

Chapter 9
The Mayor of Boxville!

A true friend is someone who thinks that you are a good egg even though he knows that you are slightly cracked.

>   Bernard Meltzer---Radio Host

In 1927 Time Magazine started the tradition of selecting a **Man of the Year** Award. The first winner in 1927 was the famous aviator Charles Lindbergh. Since then the winners have been a 'Who's Who' of famous men like Walter Chrysler, Franklin D. Roosevelt, Winston Churchill, Harry S. Truman, Charles de Gaulle, John F. Kennedy and many more.

I'd like to add someone to that list. He may not be as famous as the illustrious men on the Time Magazine list but his story will fascinate you. His name is Mackie Choice. His friends call him Mack. He is one of the best friends I have on the planet. My friendship with him is also one of the most unlikely ones on the planet.

I first met Mack on a fateful summer day in August of 2003. I was a 'green behind the ears' Executive Director of a brand new charity called the SoupMobile and Mack was the longtime Mayor of Boxville. Two men from different worlds about to collide on the glide path of life. Here is how it all went down.

In August of 2003 the SoupMobile was born and I began a new journey in my own life---a journey to feed and shelter the homeless. On that fateful August day I drove the SoupMobile feeding van into Mayor Mack's homeless camp in South Dallas. I saw a sight that absolutely amazed me. It was a city of hundreds of homes stretched out in neat rows, streets and alleys. But unlike a typical suburban neighborhood of homes which are made of brick and mortar, it was a city of large cardboard boxes. In those boxes lived a multitude of homeless men and women.

Mack was the Mayor of that encampment. Yes, THE MAYOR. Oh they may not have taken a formal vote like when voting for the Mayor of a major city, but nonetheless Mack was the Mayor. A Mayor by consensus. He ran the box town---he was the Mayor of Boxville. His job was to keep the trouble makers out, make sure the sick and hurting got treatment, help keep the camp clean and sanitary and a whole host of other official duties. And make no mistake about it, as Mayor, he was just as important to the smooth running of Boxville as Mayor Tom Leppert is to the City of Dallas. (More on Mayor Mack & Mayor Tom later).

So on that fateful August day in 2003 I drove the SoupMobile Feeding Van right up into Mayor Mack's homeless box camp. I had never heard of Mack and he didn't have a clue of who I was. I was plenty nervous as I drove into the camp. This was my first foray into feeding the homeless and I was a total rookie. As I pulled into the encampment I pulled up right next to Mack's home---it must have been divine providence. His home was more elaborate than the others. It was actually a series of large boxes that were attached---like a regular home with additions. I surmised that someone of importance must be living in that home but I never suspected it would be the Mayor.

As I got out of my van, I just stood there. I wasn't really sure what to do. Yes I had food to feed the people in the camp but I wasn't even sure if I would be accepted or even allowed to serve that day. Remember I was on their turf---this was their city.

As I stood there Mayor Mack came out of his box home and walked up to me. I could instantly see he was a man of importance. He carried himself with an air of confidence and authority. He didn't say a word---he just slowly looked me up and down. I was sweating bullets. I blurted out that I was the SoupMan and was there to feed the homeless. He didn't seem much impressed and he still didn't say a word. Now I was really worried. I thought I might just get thrown out of there. Then in a moment of divine inspiration I looked Mack right in the eye and said, "may I have your permission to serve food." He paused a moment before answering and said, "you can feed here today" with the emphasis on **_'today.'_**

Whew, that was a close call, but at least for the day I was in. I had Mayor Mack's permission to feed in Boxville that day. The next day when I came back I stuck to my mantra and said to Mayor Mack, "may I have your permission to serve food." His pause was a little shorter than the day before but his answer was the same, "you can feed here _today_." For the next few weeks we kept up the same exact dialogue. Finally one day he said, "You can feed here." The word '_today_' had been dropped from the sentence. I finally had Mayor Mack's permission to feed his people on a permanent basis. Little did I know at the time, that Mack and I would become lifelong friends.

As time went on, Mack and I got to know each other better. He knew my intentions were honorable and that I was there in his camp only to help. I had no ulterior motives and I did nothing to interfere with his Mayorship. It was his turf and I respected that. Mack on the other hand respected what I was doing and never tried to interfere with my feeding operation. Over time our friendship grew. Two men from different worlds with a mutual respect for each other. In addition to being my friend, Mack turned out to be my guardian angel. It's not all sugar and spice out on the streets and Mack knew I would need a blanket of protection.

I heard through the homeless grapevine that Mack had put the word out on the street---"you mess with the SoupMan and you are messing with me." Oh man, that's like when the GodFather puts out the word that his guy is not to be touched. Mack's proclamation gave me the breathing room I needed to build up my own reputation on the streets.

Over time I was able to build up my own credibility and now I can go virtually anywhere in Dallas where the homeless congregate and be in total safety. I am well known by the homeless, they respect me---I respect them and they know I am there to help them. But that wasn't the case when I first started. I was literally an unknown in the homeless community. I had to earn their trust and respect and establish my own rep. Mack's decree gave me the time to do just that.

As the years went by Mack and I relied on each other for a whole host of things. If he needed extra warm clothing for his people during a winter cold spell he would call upon me for help. If I was venturing into new homeless territory I would ask him to pave the way for me. If he needed help getting medical treatment for one of his city dwellers he would come to me to make it happen. If I needed help with a homeless person that was out of line, I would ask Mack to intercede. If one of Mack's people had gotten picked up in a sweep and was in jail, he would ask me to take him reading materials and maybe a little money to spend in the jail commissary. If I was shorthanded on volunteers to serve the food that day, I would ask Mack to enlist some of his people to help me. And the list went on and on.

I was there for him and he was there for me. I remember one time I showed up at his doorstep in Boxville on a bitterly cold winter night at midnight. I had gotten in a late night donation of blankets and I thought his people could use them right away. Without any hesitation he got up out of a sound sleep and for the next few hours the two of us went around to all the cardboard box houses in Boxville passing out the blankets. Two men from different worlds, working together to make a difference in the lives of the homeless in Dallas, Texas. Two friends working for a common good. It just doesn't get much better than that!

As the SoupMobile grew I dreamed of doing more for Mack. He had been homeless for 15 years, living under a bridge in South Dallas. Yes, I said 15 years. Just try to imagine that. Could you survive one year----one month—or even one week being homeless and living in a cardboard box? For most of us the answer would be---No Way! Yet Mack had survived 15 years being homeless on the streets of Dallas.

Absolutely incredible! I wanted to give Mack a paying job at the SoupMobile. He would be the perfect employee. We were already tried and true friends. We had already been partnering for years in helping the homeless and I knew he was 100% trustworthy.

However there was one small (okay large) problem. The SoupMobile operates on a shoestring and we watch every penny. We simply didn't have the money to hire Mack. Here's how God remedied that situation. It was a spring day in March 2009. I was driving the SoupMobile van. In the van with me was my Warehouse Manager and a volunteer by the name of Rusty. We had just finished serving 600 hot, hearty and healthy lunchtime meals to our homeless friends. We were on our way back to SoupMobile Headquarters but I needed to stop by Mayor Mack's Boxville encampment so I could drop off a pair of shoes he had requested for one of his people. Mack was always thinking about his people. I gave the shoes to Mack---he thanked me, we shook hands and waved to Mack as we drove off.

As I was driving I lamented how I would really like to hire Mack but we just could not afford it. I was just kind of talking out loud. Then I heard a quiet voice from the back seat say, "<u>It's done</u>." I knew it was Rusty talking but I didn't know what he was referring to. I said "what do you mean "It's done." He said "I mean it's done." I replied "what's done." He stuck to his manta and said "It's done." (I'm not making this stuff up---this is all absolutely true---just ask Rusty). For a moment I was silent and then the light bulb went off in my head and I said "do you mean you are going to sponsor Mack's salary at the SoupMobile." Rusty replied "It's done." Yep, he's a man of few words but oh can he get things done.

Rusty told me that he and his wife Betsy would sponsor Mack's salary though the end of the year---2009. So we hired Mack on April 1, 2009 and true to their word a check appeared every month from Rusty & Betsy to sponsor Mack's salary. We never had to remind them and we never sent them a bill. They said they would sponsor Mack's salary until the end of 2009 and that's just what they did. But that's not the end of the Rusty & Betsy story.

Heading into 2010 we knew the SoupMobile would be on the hook for Mack's salary. We were still pinching out pennies but there was no way we were going to let Mack go. I didn't know where we were going to find the money but I knew we had to keep Mack with us. First of all he was my good friend. Second he had a work ethic second to none. I tell my new workers, don't even think about outworking Mack----It ain't gonna happen! I tell them if they can do just half as good as Mack, I will be very pleased. Anyway back to Rusty & Betsy. The first week in January 2010 Rusty comes walking in my office and hands me an envelope. He doesn't say a word---he just hands me an envelope. I ask him "what this all about?" He says "**It's done.**" Scouts honor---that's what he said.

Well you guessed it, Rusty & Betsy had decided to keep sponsoring Mack's salary and to this day they still faithfully bring that sponsor check each month. Or as Rusty likes to say "It's done." By the way, Rusty & Betsy don't just sponsor Mack's salary each month. They are Mack's friend, they help mentor him and if you want to find Mack on Thanksgiving day, just head over to the home of Rusty & Betsy and you will see them all sitting down together enjoying Thanksgiving dinner. One final note on Rusty. He married up! Betsy is a total sweetheart. All of her friends call her Betsy but at the SoupMobile we call her Angel. Did I mention Rusty married up!

So now Mack had a job. He worked at the SoupMobile and was getting a regular paycheck. But there was a problem. Mack was still living in a cardboard box under that bridge in South Dallas. Housing is expensive in Dallas and even though Mack was getting a regular paycheck, it wasn't enough to get him off the streets. That's when SoupMobile Village came into the picture. Remember earlier in this book how I told you about the opening of our Group Men's Home in October of 2009. Guess who was the first resident we moved into that home. Oh yeah, it was Mack. Who else!

By this time Mack & I had a lot of history together. Two men from different worlds who had become fast and true friends. I never forgot how, in the early days of the SoupMobile, Mack had put the word out on the streets---"you mess with the SoupMan and you are messing with me." And what makes it more amazing is that when Mack said that, he didn't have a clue (nor did I) that someday we would be in a position to offer him a job and put a roof over his head. He didn't put out that mantle of protection for me to get anything in return. He did it because he was my friend. Mack's early protection was pivotal in giving me the time to get established on the streets with the homeless community. He was a key player in helping the SoupMobile get off the ground.

I had known all along that Mack just had to be the first person to move into SoupMobile Village. He had been loyal to me and now it was my turn to return the favor. Mack moved into the Men's Home on October 7, 2009. The word had gotten out to the local press and a reporter and photographer turned up from the Dallas Morning News. There was also TV coverage from Channel 8. This was big news---a man who had been homeless for 15 years was now getting a home of his own. The story was so big that it made the front page of the Dallas Morning News in a full feature article. At the Grand Opening of the Men's Home, Cynthia---the Channel 8 TV reporter asked Mack this question. She said to Mack, "now you have a job and a home---if you had one other wish, what would it be?" Without much hesitation Mack said "I'd like to be able to smile without being embarrassed."

You can imagine that after being homeless for 15 years, Mack's teeth were in pretty bad shape. In fact they were in terrible shape. His teeth were so bad and so infected that they would all have to be pulled out. Cynthia put out an 'On the Air' appeal for a dentist to help Mack. Almost immediately we got several dentists who called and offered to give Mack a free set of dentures. And while we were very grateful for their generous offers, I wanted more for Mack. He had always been good to me and I wanted the best for him. Removable dentures would have been okay, but I dreamed of a permanent set of teeth for Mack. That meant permanent dental implants---that meant BIG money. None of the dentists that had offered the dentures were able to help with dental implants. And there was no way the SoupMobile could foot the bill on implants---no way!

Essentially I had hit a brick wall. But as usual I turned to my ace in the hole---God. I went to God and said, "My friend Mack needs dental implants—can you help me out!" Yep, that was it---short and sweet. Generally that's how God and I communicate---pretty succinctly. He seems to be cool with it and so am I. I'm not saying my way to talk to God is the best way. I'm only saying that it seems to work for me most of the time. So you approach him in whatever way works best for you. Bottom line---when you've got a problem---talk to God about it and if you really get stuck, just call 1-800 MY GOD.

I didn't hear an immediate answer from God and I wasn't much worried about it. I knew he would figure it out for me. Or in this case, it turned out that he would prod me to figure it out. Here's how it all went down. It just so happens that I had an appointment coming up with my own personal dentist---Dr. Lee Fitzgerald. I got to thinking about it and then the light bulb went off in my head---ask Dr. Fitzgerald if he would do dental implants for Mack.

Over the years he had been my personal dentist and had supported the SoupMobile with some financial and clothing donations. I thought he was a pretty 'cool cat.' He was very particular about the dental work he did on his patients. He would not let you out of the chair if it wasn't just right. He didn't tolerate sloppy work. I have often told Lee that if he hadn't become a dentist, he could have been a master cabinet maker. He is that good with his hands.

So anyway, it was a big leap from some financial and clothing donations to doing a full mouth implant job on Mack. A leap of $60,000 dollars it turned out. Yes, you heard right---SIXTY THOUSAND dollars and I was going to ask Lee to do it pro-bono (for free). So the next time I visited his office I decided I would pop the question. That day I was just getting my teeth cleaned and he stopped in afterwards to say hi and take a quick look at my mouth to make sure everything was okay. When he was done I turned to him and asked if he had a moment to talk. He said he did. I swallowed deep and told him Mack's story. Homeless for 15 years---my good friend---his job at the SoupMobile---our first resident in the SoupMobile Village Men's Home and his wish to be able to smile without being embarrassed.

I told Dr. Fitzgerald that several dentists had already offered removable dentures but that we wanted more for Mack---permanent dental implants. Then I came right out and said, "Could you do that for Mack?" I will never forget Lee's response. He didn't say a word---he just tilted his head a little downward for a few seconds and then he turned back to me and said in a quiet voice, "I could do that." Wow, totally awesome. It reminded me of when Rusty had said "It's done." Lee simply said, "I could do that." Did I mention Wow!

And with those four simple words---"I could do that", the transformation of Mack's mouth began. It was not a simple task. Mack's old broken teeth were in extremely bad shape. His gums were so infected, that Dr. Fitzgerald said that he had not seen anything like that in his 20 plus years of practice. Over the next 12 months Mack had a series of visits for dental work. It was a major production. The old teeth had to all come out; the infection had to be treated; temporary dentures had to be crafted while

Mack's mouth was healing; then surgery to put in implant posts; then more healing; then more surgery. It took a multitude of man hours and dedication by Dr. Fitzgerald and his amazing staff.

Lee even called in outside help. A doctor to treat Mack's infection and an anesthesiologist for the surgeries. $60,000 dollars of work later and after over a year of diligent and painstaking work by Dr. Fitzgerald's team, Mack got his wish. He could now smile without being embarrassed. Now Mack had a permanent gleaming bright smile for all to see. By the way, you've all heard of Lee Majors who starred in the TV series---'The <u>Six Million</u> Dollar Man' back in 1974. We call Mack 'The <u>Sixty Thousand</u> Dollar Man!'

Through it all we never got one bill from Lee—not one. At the beginning of the process he had said "I could do that" and that was that. He gave his word and never flinched. And even though Mack's mouth and the infection were the worst he had ever seen, he never hinted of backing out, never said this is too much and never complained. My grateful thanks to Dr. Fitzgerald, his fabulous staff and all the outside helpers he brought in to make it all happen. In a world where it sometimes seems that people only care about themselves, Lee is a shining example of the love of Jesus in action. And did I mention that he is a 'cool cat.'

Oh, and let's not forget that earlier in this chapter I said I would tell you more about the Mayor Mack & Mayor Tom story. At the SoupMobile's Christmas event in 2009 these two Mayors got together to make a real difference in the lives of the homeless in Dallas. Two men from opposite worlds coming together to serve the ones Jesus called the 'least of these.' The Mayor of Boxville---Mack Choice and the Mayor of Dallas---Tom Leppert. Two men coming together to make it a magical Christmas for 500 homeless people.

It all took place at the Christmas banquet that the SoupMobile puts on for our 500 homeless guests on Christmas Eve. At most banquets it's the big muckety mucks who are sitting down to the fancy dinner and being served by elegant waiters. At the SoupMobile banquet it's just the opposite. 'WE' are the ones doing the serving and it's the homeless that are being served. We treat them like Kings & Queens. Fine china, elegant tablecloths, soft music and top of the line food. At the banquet Mayor Mack and Mayor Tom were both dressed in elegant tuxedoes as they served the homeless at adjacent tables. Two men from different worlds who thought it NOT beneath themselves to serve 500 homeless men and women at Christmas.

As both Mayor's served, the news photographers clicked off picture after picture. A reporter from the Dallas Morning News chronicled every detail. Local TV stations captured the magical moments on film for the evening news. This was a big story---The Mayor of Boxville and the Mayor of Dallas joined arm in arm in serving their fellow man. Interestingly enough, neither man seemed much interested in all the fuss. They were both focused on being of service. Neither man came to be served---they came to <u>serve others</u>. I'm very confident that Jesus was looking down and smiling at their efforts.

Now let's come full circle--- Mack and the SoupMan! We were strangers when we first met in 2003 but I never thought of Mack as a 'client.' He was never a 'number' in our computer. He, like all the homeless men and women that we deal with, are precious children of the Lord most high. Did I know at that fateful first meeting in Boxville in 2003 that it would turn into a lifelong friendship? No, I really didn't have a clue. But God knew---<u>HE</u> knew that we would go from "you can feed here <u>today</u>" to a friendship that I deeply treasure.

As a young boy growing up in Detroit, Michigan I could have never imagined that I would grow up to be the SoupMan and become lifelong friends with Mack---the Mayor of Boxville. But it seems we serve a God that plans ahead. HE had it all planned out from the very beginning! God Is <u>NOT</u> On Vacation!

Chapter 10
Is This <u>Your</u> Moment?

Any life, no matter how long and complete it may be, is made up of a **<u>single moment</u>**---the moment in which a person finds out, once and for all, who they are.

                Jorge Luis Borges---Author

I believe that life is a series of moments. I believe that every once in a rare while, God sends us a **single moment** that can become 'our' defining moment.

A moment where we have to decide. Is this the time I step up and start making a real difference in the world? Is this the time I begin reaching out to my fellowman with love, caring, and compassion? Is this 'my' time to start reaching out in faith to those in need.

We can't all be Mother Teresa's but in our own unique way we can make a real difference in this world. Within each one of us God has planted a seed. In my childhood of hunger he planted a seed that grew into the SoupMan.

What seed has he planted in you? What's your gift to this world? Is it the giving of yourself, your time, your finances and your love? I pray it's all of these.

So I ask you?

IS THIS <u>YOUR</u> MOMENT?

Is this your moment for your seed to sprout. You've read this book right up to this last chapter. Are you going to put this book down without vowing to do something? Can you close this book and just walk away? Is God handing you that <u>single moment</u> right now? What better time than right now to start making a difference in the world you live in!

Maybe your heart is saying yes, but your head says no. Are your fearful that you don't have enough time in the day to make a difference? Let the words of Jackson Brown guide you---"Don't say you don't have enough time. You have exactly the same number of hours per day that were given to Helen Keller, Louis Pasteur, Michaelangelo, Mother Teresa, Leonardo da Vinci, Thomas Jefferson and Albert Einstein."

Will you begin to make your mark on this world? Are you ready to step out in faith and watch God guide you every step of the way? Are you ready to work without a net---at least a visible net? Are you ready to put it all on the line?

So I ask you again.

IS THIS <u>YOUR</u> MOMENT?

You may be asking---How? Just how can I start making a difference? I don't even know where to begin. You could start volunteering somewhere.

And it doesn't have to be at the SoupMobile. You could even start a SoupKitchen of your own. I routinely get emails from around the country and around the world from people who have heard or read about the SoupMobile. They contact me for tips and advice on starting a SoupKitchen in their part of the world. A few months ago I got an email from Australia---the country we call down under, asking for help in starting a soupkitchen. A country half way around the world, but somehow they had heard about the SoupMobile.

Maybe for you starting a soupkitchen is NOT the seed God has planted in you. Maybe the seed he planted is for you to volunteer at a soupkitchen. Again, it doesn't have to be the SoupMobile---but if you are local to the Dallas area, it could be! For more information about volunteering at the SoupMobile, go to www.soupmobile.org

So I ask you one final time?

IS THIS <u>YOUR</u> MOMENT?

If you do come and volunteer at the SoupMobile, remember to lead with love. Yes, come and join the

SoupMan & his fabulous SoupTeam on the front lines as we serve food to our homeless friends.

Come and help mentor our family of men and women who live in our group homes in SoupMobile Village.

Come and volunteer at our Christmas event called Celebrate Jesus. By the way, if you volunteer at our Christmas event, it will NOT be the best volunteer opportunity of the year for you---it will be the best volunteer opportunity of your life. When you see the tears in the eyes of the homeless and the smiles on their faces, your heart will be touched as it has never been before.

Come and share in our dream of reaching out to the ones Jesus called the 'least of these.' Come with the Love of Jesus in your heart. And if you come, be prepared to throw Conventional Wisdom out the door. Be prepared to fasten your seatbelts as you take the ride of your life. Be ready to crawl out on a limb with us and watch the miracles of God pour out.

Come knowing that the SoupMan will ask you to give of yourself and then he will ask you to give even more of your love, caring and compassion. Finally be prepared for your heart to be filled with the love and joy that we all receive as we go about our 'Fathers business.'

Come and make it **your moment** to start making a real difference in this world.

FINAL NOTE: If reading this book does nothing more than galvanize you to start making a real difference in your corner of world, then my work is done. So wherever you are on this planet, my prayer is that you will see this as 'your moment' to start making a difference in the lives of the ones Jesus called the 'least of these.'

Godspeed!

May the Lord bless and keep you.

Signed, David Timothy, a.k.a. The SoupMan

Executive Director---SoupMobile Inc.

Publishing Notes

If you enjoyed this book,

God Is <u>NOT</u> On Vacation!

you might also enjoy reading the SoupMan's first book titled, **Is God On Vacation?**

Did you feel blessed by this book? Did it make an impact on you? Was your heart touched? If so, might you consider Paying it Forward. Might a friend or a loved one also be blessed by reading this book. Please take a moment and give it prayerful consideration.

Additional information on how to acquire any of the SoupMan's book's can be found by going to www.soupmobile.org. A portion of the proceeds of each book sale goes directly to feeding the homeless.

If you felt blessed by the book, please consider writing a review of the book with the online book seller that offers the book, amazon.com. More information can be found at www.soupmobile.org. Be well and may the Lord bless you and yours.

Message from the SoupMan

Did you enjoy this book? Was your heart touched? Did you feel blessed? If so, might you consider writing a review of the book. As you know the more favorable reviews a book receives---the more sales it makes---& thus the more food we can buy for the homeless. Since the book is available exclusively at amazon.com, that is where you would write the review.

Writing a review is easy. Go to amazon.com and type in the name of the book. David has written two books. The 1st book is titled: <u>Is God on Vacation</u> and the 2nd book is titled: <u>God is NOT on Vacation</u>. Then click on *Write Your Own Review* and write whatever your heart leads you to write. One caution! In the box where you actually write the review, be sure to click on *Insert a Product Link*. When you do that it will bring up my book along with several other books with similar titles. You will need to click on my specific book title to make sure your review goes to the correct book. God bless you and yours.

signed, David Timothy, a.k.a. The SoupMan

If you want to contact the SoupMan, you can email him at:

<u>david@soupmobile.org</u>

David personally reads all of his emails and he makes it a point to respond to each and every one of them.

If you want to receive the SoupMobile's free quarterly Newsletter, go to www.soupmobile.org and click on NEWSLETTER SIGN UP.

For more information about the SoupMobile, go to: www.soupmobile.org

Or call the SoupMobile at 1-800-375-5022

Made in the USA
Charleston, SC
01 December 2010